The Principle Approach

THE KEYS TO RECOVERY

BY DR. DAVID SUTTON
WITH FOREWORD BY DICK SMOTHERS

the Peppertree Press
Sarasota, Florida

The Twelve Steps are reprinted with permission of Alcholics Anonymous World Services Inc. Permission to reprint the Twelve Steps does not mean that AA has reviewed or approved the contents of this publication, nor that AA agrees with the views expressed herein. AA is a program of recovery from alcoholism *only* — use of the Twelve Steps in commection with other programs that are patterned after AA, but address other problems, or in any other non-AA context, does not imply otherwise. The Twelve Steps of AA are taken from *Alcoholics Anonymous* (fourth edition), and published by AA World Services Inc., New York, N.Y. 59-60. Reprinted with permission. AA Copyright 2001

Unless otherwise indicated, all Scripture quotations are taken from the *King James Version* of the Bible.

For information regarding permission,
call 941-922-2662 or contact us at our website:
www.peppertreepublishing.com or write to:
the Peppertree Press, LLC.
Attention: Publisher
1269 First Street, Suite 7
Sarasota, Florida 34236

ISBN: 978-1-61493-000-6

Library of Congress Number: 2011934706

Printed in the U.S.A.

Printed August 2011

To order additional copies you can contact us at:

Website: www.thekeystorecovery.com
Email: info@thekeystorecovery.com

Write to us: **Dr. David Sutton**
The Keys to Recovery
P.O. Box 3917
Sarasota, Florida 34230

This book is dedicated to Brad Caswell,

my friend, mentor and Recovery Sponsor for over 25 years.

Brad has been sober for 52 years.

He is known as "The Fiddler Man" playing his violin

from the stage with the original Hank Williams to

The Imperial Symphony Orchestra.

You can find him at www.TheKeysToRecovery.com ,

in our option called

"Ask the Fiddler Man" where you can place

your questions about addictions.

ACKNOWLEDGEMENTS

A sincere thanks to the people who helped me put this
book together:

Lisa Clift for the gift of many hours of writing and editing.

Major Phillip Murphy for your encouragement to write.

To my friend Bob for your amazing support.

Thanks to the folks at Peppertree Press for your help and
for your professional and personal approach.

For all those who have been in recovery with me for all
these years.

And of course to Lori, who puts up with me daily.

We pray that this book will be part of the recovery
process for many around the world. Thanks be to God,
who causes us to triumph in life!

What transcends David Sutton's infectious enthusiasm and personality is his message and world-class recovery based programs that are changing lives and communities. He's the real deal. His care for people, social services and education, all wrapped in his personal blend of knowledge, experience, intensity and eccentricities, is what makes him a 'game changer' in the recovery world. It takes Intensity, Knowledge, Persistence, Personality, and most of all a huge affinity for the people and lives that he touches. David Sutton, his message and program is the 'tri-fecta'. Meet him, read his work, let him engage you or your organization and you'll see for yourself. As always more will be revealed....

Tom Garrett, Professor
University of Tampa

Learn to Fish Recovery Center for Women""If you have had the pleasure of knowing David Sutton personally and witnessing the wonderful and powerful ministry he has to the drug and alcohol addicted, then this book is a must read.

If this is your first introduction to Dr. Sutton, then you are in for a wonderful surprise. Enjoy, learn, minister!"

Father Jim Nilon, Episcopal Priest
Throne of Grace Drug and Alcohol Ministry

From pen to paper, Dr. Sutton has a way of explaining the principles that make me want to do better for myself; from my relationship with God, to the wonderful messages of hope that I am privileged to carry to others. This is a wonderful tool for those just starting out in recovery and for those of us whose life is good and getting better.

Wonderful book!

Roger L. Hanabarger
Retired and Still Sober

David is a funny guy, he goes around starting fires! Watch him sometime as he gathers up dried broken lives, dead stuff from all over our city. Most people just walk by them without any thought. Yet David gathers and simply loves. The power of the Spirit is still at work bringing dead things to life through people like David, who sees the possibilities in what most people see as impossible.

Pastor Kirk Zahniser
First Nazarene Church

Dr. Sutton is one of those angels that fly very low – and we are fortunate that he flies low in our community. His work with Sarasota's homeless population is not only results-oriented, it is grounded in compassion and a fundamental recognition of our shared humanity. Dr. Sutton calls us all to be better individuals in building a collective community.

Kelly Kirschner, Mayor
Sarasota, Florida

Dr. David Sutton has been a powerful influence in my life and the lives of thousands. I am grateful for his friendship and the opportunities he has provided in my life to minister to others. We have him speak frequently and he knocks it out of the park every time. I am confident that this book will impact your life, and strengthen your faith.

Alan Tobiason
Celebrate Recovery, Suncoast Church

David's principle based programs are life changing events for the participants, their families, and the Sarasota community. The Jail Pod Program is proven to reduce recidivism. The VIPER and CRP programs help graduates to achieve sobriety, reunite with families, become employed, and obtain housing. As a result of these programs there are fewer impaired individuals on the streets of Sarasota, and fewer arrests for alcohol or drug violations. You can see God's hand in the miracles that are occurring in these programs. *I will tell you the truth, whatever you did for one of the least of these brothers of mine, you did for me.* (Matthew 25).

Captain Paul K. Sutton,
Sarasota Police Department

When you watch David Sutton work so enthusiastically with people and organizations, you cannot help but notice that what you are really seeing is the mind, heart, and hand of God at work through him! This book is the culmination of years of experience – but just as important, it is the culmination of years of training and inspiration from God's own Holy Spirit. David's book will enrich and empower all who take it to heart.

Pastor David B. McCoy
River's Edge Community Church

"If your fond of priceless information, a quick wit and deep belly laugh's... you'll love this book! David Sutton's interpretation and explanation of the 12 step's greatly influenced the quality of my recovery."

Sabrina Crain-Sweeney, CEO

I have had the pleasure of watching my friend Dr David Sutton, offer hope to those who I would consider hopeless, by his example he has instilled compassion where there was none and has inspired faith, that through God, they have a choice to change themselves and have a better life. God is smiling down on David and is blessing everything he is doing.

Dudley Carson, Realtor
Siesta Key, Florida

I would recommend this book to anyone interested in a very enthusiastic and honest approach to recovery. David Sutton has a wonderful way of inspiring new comers and those that have been at a stand still in recovery. His approach to the principles of life is awesome!

Coleen A. Hanabarger
Retired in Recovery

What do the 12 STEP'S MEAN TO ME ? L I F E ... They are the highway to happiness !!! I want to tell you what the step's have given me & taught me today !!!

I have learned how to apply these steps in my life. The teaching and mentoring support I have received from Dr. Sutton have changed my life. I have learned the process of how to stay clean and sober and more importantly have found the power of a loving God to make this happen. If you want to have a life that is truly free, this is the book you need to read!

Patrick Lincoln

The Scripture says, "Jesus went about all the cities and villages, teaching... preaching...and healing..." (Matthew 9:35). This reflects Dr. David Sutton's heart and is evidenced not only by words but by action. The impact of his ministry in our community is nothing short of astounding. I am thankful for his friendship.

Pastor Will Caguiat
Celebrate Recovery

For over thirty years, Dr. David Sutton's insightful expertise has affected people suffering from substance abuse to seek new lifestyles. Destructive behaviors become replaced by personal restoration. His unique blend of humor and compassion stirs you to laugh out loud and sometimes cry. This inspiring book is certain to leave an enduring imprint in your mind, while captivating your heart! The Recovery community has an exciting new tool."

G.A. Caviness, Nurse
Sarasota, Florida

This is not just another step book. David Sutton writes with humor and passion about living the principles of recovery. Using his own personal struggles as well as the heartfelt stories of recovery. David both teaches us and helps us celebrate life in the sunlight of the spirit.

Maribeth Ditmars
Author, Christopher's Journey

David inspires me by his will, strength and relentless passion for life and people. This book reflects that passion and has become a reference guide to practice and live these principles everyday.

Don Quehl
(Tennessee Don)
Retired Proctor and Gamble Training Coordinator

Book Review

"As a retired professional in the Addictions field I thought it might be of some value to you for me to write a review based on my opportunity to read "The Principle Approach" prior to its publication.

"Dr David Sutton's new addition to the literature of addictions and recovery - - "The Principle Approach" - - produces exactly what it promises in the sub-title: A set of Keys to Recovery and breaking free from the cycles of addiction. Clearly written, the volume (which is accompanied by an optional series of worksheets and DVD's that can stand on it's own) is what many Recovery texts promise to be, but are not. This text is of value to people newly in recovery as well as to those who have spent a number of years in the halls."

"By pairing each of the time-tested 12 Steps of Recovery, with one principle or more from current professional research and practice standards, Sutton gives people in recovery, as well as those who love and counsel them, firm scientific backup for the standard steps to which he cleaves without question or exception. Sutton minces no words; he is a hard liner and proud of it. By the time I finished the book I had a feeling he might be on a first name basis with the God of his understanding and that this was a Deity who had more than his share of compassion for "drunks". Additionally, Sutton had made abundantly clear the psychological principles on which each of the Steps is based. This is the "Why It Works" that is foundational to How It Works; something indescribably valuable in early recovery when it sometimes seems that the "shoulds" come fast and furious with not many "whys" to be found."

"The material is presented in easy to digest segments of no more than ten pages or so; most accompanied by convenient summaries of the major points. Although this may seem like a minor point to people unfamiliar with addictions recovery, everyone who has struggled through the months of early recovery in which a formerly agile brain is suddenly afflicted with, as best, one or another form of ADHD, will understand the importance of this formatting feature. The joy of the sense of completion when you realize that page nine is the end of a section; sections that in other traditionally formatted books, you were beginning to think would continue past receipt of your first Social Security check."

"Dr. David Sutton is unapologetically ambitious in the width of his scope, offering chapter and verse on everything from getting sober through the pitfalls of the sponsor/sponsee relationship which is designed to support addicts though the rougher parts of the journey. Something of a Recovery Celebrity with extensive experience running treatment programs in the South Florida area, Sutton makes "The Principle Approach" pretty much equivalent to having coffee with him after a meeting; maybe after a lot of meetings. So long as the reader knows this is "back in the day" based traditional recovery, unadorned by any New Age philosophy, reading this book can't be a wrong move; especially if you are at the disadvantage of not living in South Florida where you could meet the man himself."

Edith A. Cheitman, Ph.D., MSW

"I've been in the addiction field for over 30 years and never a real strong fan of the AA model until I heard Dr. David Sutton present the Twelve Steps as only he can. I was so impressed that I immediately attempted to have him do something for the Program I'm affiliated with; the Stout Street Foundation in Commerce City Colorado. A long term (2 years) substance abuse program that had, in the past, only a peripheral relationship with AA.

Although, we've been around for 35 years we will be incorporating this material into our program as soon as it is available! The way he presents the 12 steps and their corresponding principles makes an impact. Instead of a dry rendition of the Steps they come alive in his presentation. After many weeks of sitting in David's classes I asked if he had ever planned on video taping his presentation for wide distribution to the addiction community. His reply "Interesting that you should ask", already working on it. It is with great pleasure that I give this material my highest recommendation as a worthy addition to the materials that help addicts, regardless of their substance of choice, the necessary tools to facilitate recovery."

Read this book or invite him to come speak; you will not be disappointed!

Dr. Kenneth G. Wilson,
Chairman, Board of Directors
Stout Street Foundation, Inc.

FOREWORD

By Dick Smothers

I first met David Sutton in a room that was SRO; that's what all performers want to see when they take the stage for a performance. It's what they always hope for, but few achieve it on a regular basis. SRO stands for "Standing Room Only," for those of you who might be wondering. To do SRO on a regular basis it might mean that you're the newest and hottest thing or might mean you have been around for decades and have survived the highs and lows of countless successes and excesses and somehow have survived and your loyal fans can't get enough of you.

When I walked into David's room, it felt like I was in the room that had the hottest ticket in town. Standing Room Only! When David started to do his presentation my mind told me that this guy could be one of the blue collar comics. He sounded country, easy going and sort of just talking with you, just to get your focus and help you get ready to start paying attention, and then some funny stories or jokes. He utilizes all the important skills of the top comics, but he's much more. His timing is great. If he does a duck joke, his body becomes the duck. He looks like a duck walks like a duck and quacks like a duck. He gets his laughs. He may stop at any time and ask what did I just say? He does this a lot. We all know we must pay attention. We all yell back the answer until he is satisfied that we got it. I'm not sure why, but it feels good yelling back together as a group. Yes there are many laughs, but the main point is recovery—the message that we can get our lives back and they can be new and better than before.

He sometimes sings, and very well in a soft country style that can bring a tear to even the hardest of the hard, for we know he sings of what he knows and where he has been, and we can relate as we go to our own personal secret private places. He knows—and we know—that we don't have to live in our addictions anymore. This recovery program, of which the 12 Steps are foundational, can set us free when we apply its principles in all aspects of our lives.

For many of the people in the room, this is their last chance at life. They are not your typical comedy club audience. Their lives had become unmanageable and most have nowhere to turn. They have come from all walks of life looking for hope. Most will come to believe in a power greater than themselves, something that could restore the sanity in their lives. Many have made a decision to turn their wills and their lives over to the care of God—bottom line—and they're ready to go to any length to get and stay sober.

That is the first step…a step to a life that can and will be beyond your wildest dreams if you follow these Simple 12 Steps and their corresponding principles. It is a life beyond description. The people in the room truly were the fortunate ones, for David just might be running the best recovery program in the country. He motivates. As the class continues, I feel the room take on a collective energy, I sense their spirit, their hope and their belief that David's program will, if they truly want it and will work for it, give them a life they all desperately want, the life they were meant to have.

I know this also was true for another person in the room, not too different than these individuals, many years ago. It was me: I was one of them. I am still one of them, and I always will be among their ranks. I'm proud of my friend David Sutton, for I believe he is doing God's work.

In my recovery the 12 Steps are fundamental. One can't read them and understand them intellectually and be cured. They are not to be raced through and finished. I believe they should be learned through the heart, from the inside out. If you do that, eventually you will be a new and a much better human being. That's what the 12 Steps are all about, to make you a better human being, and I believe that's what my God wants of me. Life for me has never been better and thank Goodness its progress not perfection. A wise person said that "wisdom becomes knowledge when it is personal experience." David teaches what he has experienced, what he knows. He has been there...and I can relate to what he says.

I like what's in this book. When I read it, I felt as if I was back in his classroom. I see the faces, hear the sounds, feel the energy, and sense the anticipation. Then I hear the softening of the sounds, then a quietness filling the room and then finally I hear a gentle voice telling you the truth. It really doesn't matter what he asks or says because he's already got you!!!!

Dick Smothers is an American actor, comedian, composer, and musician. He is best known for being half of the musical comedy team the Smothers Brothers with his older brother Tom.

INTRODUCTION

When my oldest son David was about 5 years old, he loved cars and trucks of all kinds, especially racecars. Money was tight, but I had a plan to take him to the Stock car races. I put some of my paycheck aside each week for months, and we talked every night about the plan.

As the weeks went by, his excitement grew and finally the day came that we had anticipated for so long! I hadn't been to many racetracks in my life, so I was just as pumped up as my son. We arrived at the track early and waited in line anxiously for tickets. When we finally had our tickets and programs in hand, we went in the gate and began to make our rounds to the food counters for popcorn, Coke, and cotton candy. From there we went to the souvenir stand and bought a hat, a flag, and a toy Stock car.

We headed up the ramp into the arena loaded down with enough stuff to guarantee we looked like typical newcomers to the races. When we got to the top, we were about 5 feet from the chain link fence that separated us from the track. When the first group of about 15 cars roared past us, the wind blew dust and exhaust fumes in our eyes, and the noise level deafened our ears. We were shocked to say the least.

David was scared out of his wits and began to scream, "It's too loud, it's too loud. I'm scared! Take me home."

I picked him up and told him it would be OK, we would go up in the stands and it wouldn't be so loud. With 200 people watching my balancing act, I moved David and all of our stuff high up to lessen the noise and commotion. In the confusion, we had lost the toy car, a flag, and one of the programs. Then David noticed we were sitting on open bleachers, and it was a long way to the ground.

He screamed almost as loud as the first time, "We're up too high. We're going to fall!"

I tried to settle him down, but my words didn't work. I picked him up along with the soda, popcorn, and souvenirs. Going down, we stumbled over the same people we had stepped around coming up. I'm sure they were glad we were moving. Later, we were almost in the front again, and we were down to the box of popcorn, a Coke, and a program. Then the cars roared by again. David begged me to please take him home one last time, and now with only the single program in hand we left the arena. The whole ordeal was about an hour from beginning to end, and we were back in the car.

As we pulled out of the parking lot, I was holding back tears of disappointment and David was busy looking through the program book at the pictures of all the Stock cars. The next day at church he told everyone, young and old alike, that his dad had taken him to the car races. It was interesting to me at the time that he had no idea what he had missed. He was happy just having the program to read and show off to others.

What I had planned for him was so much bigger than he had been able to understand or to experience. He settled to go home with a program in hand because he couldn't see the big picture. Many people do that when it comes to recovery; they settle for less because they don't see the big picture. Like David, they are afraid to put faith into their Father and trust that He has a plan.

This story has a message, and it sets the stage as we start down the pathway of breaking the cycle of addictions. One of my goals is to show you that God has a bigger plan for you than to just help you quit your addiction. His objective is for you to have a wonderful life full of blessings. Don't miss the main event and settle for just reading the program!

You can work any 12 Step program out there and maintain

some degree of sobriety, which at the lowest level is to just stop using a substance or engaging in an addictive behavior. However, without a properly structured approach and faith it's easy to miss out on the most important part of the process—attaining life principles that fundamentally change your beliefs and allow you to live a happy existence connected with God. The principles associated with the 12 Steps are the keys to making permanent changes and safeguarding you from falling back into old behaviors.

You can receive unexpected and unforeseen help when you ask for assistance with the right intentions—and sometimes Divine Intervention is channeled through the grace of others in your life. After reading this book, I hope that you will become one of those people. My message to you at the outset of this journey is: **God can and will remove the desire for alcohol or drugs or anything else that is destroying your life.** Once the obsession is removed, you will need to change your lifestyle to stay free. The best way to achieve this goal is by working some kind of program that includes a step process that incorporates learning and adhering to some basic life principles. Whatever addiction you are fighting you can win if you learn the tools necessary to fight back.

My belief in this approach is based on 25 years of teaching in treatment programs and jails, as well as training ministers and certified addictions counselors over more than two decades. Additionally, I have spent more than 30 years participating in the meetings of different recovery fellowships, which has exposed me to hundreds of thousands of individuals working to break the cycle of addictions. With this experience behind me, I can assure you that the approach outlined in the following chapters works if you work it.

This book is about life principles in recovery and how to apply them with enthusiasm! You need passion in your recovery. The number one reason people relapse in their addictions is because they develop an attitude of apathy, which always seems to lead to lethargic efforts to maintain sobriety and lead a healthy life. In my experience, when people reenter their addictions they have disregarded what they have learned in recovery and return to their old ways of thinking and acting. ***The first step in relapse is ignoring what you already know.*** It is my observation that most of the time they also have stopped going to meetings. Ask them why they are no longer are attending and invariably they will tell you they became indifferent and lazy or distracted by the good things that sobriety has brought them.

Enthusiasm actually generates a chemical change inside of your brain that helps to combat negative emotions. It releases endorphins, and that creates a sense of well being. I had this experience firsthand when I got sober in 1980. It was at a Sunday night meeting in the suburbs of Cleveland, Ohio, and in that group I found the enthusiasm and excitement I am talking about here. As a result, it created an energy release that helped jumpstart me on the path of recovery.

It was a huge gathering of almost 200 people. Members would start setting up the room around 6:00 p.m. by making coffee and greeting people. The meeting would start at 8:00 p.m. with a hubbub of activity, and then the chairman for the month would introduce the speaker with great excitement. After about an hour, the meeting would open up for comments and those who wanted to share would stand up and talk, expressing their feelings about what was said. People were gregarious and funny, and it was infectious. It would go until 10:00 p.m. most nights, and then there was coffee and doughnuts. Sometimes the group didn't break up until midnight!

The members were so enthusiastic about the meeting that as a newcomer I wanted to help clean up every week. At one of my first few meetings I went in the kitchen and got a rag to help wash some of the dishes. Somebody quickly stopped me and said that job belonged to somebody else. Then I went out and picked up a broom, and I had the same experience. People were waiting in line to do service work at that meeting. Now that's passion!

If you connect to this type of energy your chances for success in recovery will be great because it results in emotional entrainment.

The word entrain can be defined as drawing something along as a current does in a river. In this case, the positive energy of the group was like a wave that drew me into a healthier emotional state. It was much easier to maintain a positive attitude as a part of this group than to try swimming upstream in recovery on my own.

With the right mindset and spiritual direction, the steps and their associated principles can liberate you from addictions. However, the specific approach you take is an important consideration. Some people believe you only have to work the process once and you've got it, while others say you have to work this every day for the rest of your life. "For the rest of my life" was too much for me to grasp when I finally got sober. I had been relapsing for seven years, and at that time I couldn't understand the concept of "don't drink forever," let alone work the process every day I have left on this earth. This never-ending task without closure was overwhelming.

The only idea I could comprehend at first was one day at a time, and later I understood that there was a reasonable goal in working the steps—that was attaining the principles, which were derived from the Four Absolutes developed in the early days of recovery: Honesty, Purity, Unselfishness, and Love. These principles are guideposts, and as you learn to apply them they will begin to have a positive impact in your life. They are not new, but they are timeless and should become integral keystones in your recovery process.

Here are the 12 Steps, in their original form,
listed with the principles upon which they are founded.

1. We admitted we were powerless over alcohol—and that our lives had become unmanageable.
2. Came to believe that a Power greater than ourselves could restore us to sanity.
3. Made a decision to turn our will and our lives over to the care of God as *we understood Him*
4. Made a fearless and searching moral inventory of ourselves.

5. Admitted to God, to ourselves, and to another human being the exact nature of our wrongs.

6. Were entirely ready to have God remove all these defects of character.

7. Humbly asked Him to remove our shortcomings.

8. Made a list of all persons we had harmed, and became willing to make amends to them all.

9. Made direct amends to such people wherever possible, except when to do so would injure them or others.

10. Continued to take personal inventory and when we were wrong promptly admitted it.

11. Sought through prayer and meditation to improve our conscious contact with God as *we understood Him*, praying only for knowledge of His will for us and the power to carry that out.

12. Having had a spiritual awakening as a result of these steps, we tried to carry this message to alcoholics, and to practice these principles in all our affairs.

Here are the principles that I have found that best match the step process. There are many different versions of these. PRINCIPLES:

1	**Honesty**	7	**Humility**
2	**Hope**	8	**Brotherly Love**
3	**Faith**	9	**Discipline**
4	**Courage**	10	**Perseverance**
5	**Integrity**	11	**Awareness of God**
6	**Willingness**	12	**Service**

Some are discovery steps. You are taking the denial out of the addiction, and during the process you will discover the true nature of your problems. Some are recovery steps. In this phase, you are blocking the reoccurring behaviors that will produce more negative memories. You adopt a new approach to life that will allow you to eliminate the character defects that have caused pain and/or relapse over the years. Some provide a process that will break the repetitive cycle of stress that can build up to a point that will cause you to fall into old thinking patterns and even depression. They make sure you will not miss your chance to live a full and happy life. Finally, some are maintenance steps. This is where you use God's help to grow and live a life free from addiction.

I firmly believe most people wind up addicted because they don't understand how to live by healthy principles. You probably grew up like I did, without really grasping or connecting to life values. Or maybe you connected with them, and then you started drinking and using drugs and you lost those ethics. That's why the main objective of this book is to show you that principles are the keys to making lasting and effective changes in your life through a recovery program based on principle not opinion.

Many people don't understand principles; they only understand rules. Let me explain. If you run into a rule, you can break the rule. As a result, there may be a consequence or there may not be an effect. However, when you run into a principle, it doesn't break—you do. A principle is a fundamental, primary, or general law or truth that operates at a universal level in your life. When you start violating rules long enough, eventually you compromise the associated principle and your life turns upside down.

For example, let's look at a 35 mph speed limit in a school zone. The rule is set for a specific time and place for a reason, and if you go 45 miles per hour in the school zone during the designated hours you will break the rule. You may do this two or three times and not get caught, but then one day a police officer stops you and you get a ticket. If this happens enough times you will violate the governing principle of safe driving and lose your license. Safe driving is a principle that applies everywhere as opposed to just a rule that is made up for a particular place in a specific setting. In the case of recovery, a rule is to attend a meeting every day. You may break the rule and miss one here and there, but miss enough meetings and you will violate the principle that meeting attendance is critical to maintaining sobriety. As a result, you will revert to your old behaviors and relapse.

As we get ready to dive into the principles, I want you to

contemplate the difference between floating in a swamp and riding the current on a river. In a swamp, water pools up and overflows because there are no set boundaries. It is murky and stagnant. A river is different because it has banks. There is a channel that the water runs through to reach a destination. The power of a river is in its movement, and that flow is a result of its boundaries. The same is true in recovery. If you use the principles to set your own personal boundaries you will have a purpose in life and your recovery will move forward on a positive current. If you don't have life principles, you can be assured that you are destined to keep swimming in the same murky, dark swamps over and over again.

It's time to get your life moving again! Let's begin now, one principle at a time.

Welcome
To Your New Life!

" The first step to relapse

is ignoring what

you already know "

David Sutton

CONTENTS

A drunk was in a bar and there was a dog sitting next to him.

A guy walked in and sat down next to the drunk.

He said, "Hey buddy, does your dog bite?"

The drunk slurred, "Noooo, my dog doesn't bite."

They guy reached down to pet the dog,

and the dog dug his teeth into his hand.

He said, "I thought you said your dog doesn't bite."

"Well, that's not my dog," the drunk replied.

CHAPTER 1
HONESTY

When I was a little boy, I never really learned the meaning of honesty. As a child I wouldn't have understood how important this principle wass in developing a solid spiritual foundation in life. I was too busy paying attention to other things like most kids do. The difference was that much of what I had to watch were not age appropriate, like the raging arguments that were ongoing between my parents. I was trying to make sure I didn't get in the middle of them, so I was too distracted to learn social skills, study, or even fun; self esteem, spirituality, or how to operate from a position of hope in my life was not even part of the equation. Even though I attended a church where prayer was practiced, I wasn't speaking to God about learning the principles I needed to guide my life because I was busy praying, "Please God, don't let the fight be about me tonight."

As a result of my childhood home environment and upbringing, I lacked the ability to develop a normal relationship with another human being later in life. When I would try, I got hurt immediately. When I opened up my heart and told the truth it always seemed to backfire, so I learned how to lie to survive. I worked on dishonesty and built my life around fabrication and fantasy. I had to keep in place the dream world reputation I had created in my mind; I put on like a costume for all to see—a mask that was designed to keep other people away. I was on the outside looking in;

I began to live in this fantasy world that I created, and it ultimately was fueled by my addiction to alcohol and other substances.

I was unable to break this cycle until I entered into recovery and learned how to become honest with God, myself, and others. Grasping the principle of honesty changed my life because it started the process of breaking free from self centeredness and denial, and it provided the keystone to build healthy relationships.

> **Step 1:** *We admitted we were powerless over alcohol—that our lives had become unmanageable.*

PRINCIPLE: HONESTY

Growing up without principles is dangerous because when you have no values you remain juvenile in the way you perceive life. Your body grows up, but your emotions do not follow in its footsteps. You fool yourself and become dishonest about your life. That's definitely what happened to me, and if you're an addict you probably are in the same boat. Whether you sink or swim in recovery will depend on your ability to master the first step and incorporate the principle of honesty in your life. Hold on to it tightly, and it will become your life preserver.

To master this principle, you first must come to an understanding of what it is to be "constitutionally incapable of being honest." I've found that there is something about the general character of people who are active in addictions that prohibits them from being honest. Ultimately, it comes down to ingrained belief systems that unwittingly block their true understanding of what honesty means.

Never have I seen a person fail who has completely followed through with this journey. Those who do not recover from addiction are people who cannot or will not get honest. Usually these are men and women who are in their constitution and belief system, incapable of being **honest** with themselves.

This analogy will help you to better understand this concept. The United States Constitution is the framework for the country and an expression of what citizens believe and support as a whole. It represents the concepts and philosophies that hold up the internal workings of the democracy. The same applies for individual people. Deep down inside of each person are all of the things that he or she believes, and they are written in a personal constitution that is embedded in the neural network of the brain. For addicts, this information has been shaped in such a way that it doesn't allow for honesty. If there's a problem with the United States Constitution, it is amended. Similarly, if there's something wrong with your internal constitution, then it's time to alter it and change the foundation of your beliefs.

You are not defined by what you feel. You are defined by what you believe. What you believe makes you who you are. This might be confusing, so let's look at it another way: What you believe and what you feel are not the same things. Your feelings may change easily from moment to moment or situation to situation, but you will need a strong outside stimulus to initiate a significant change to your core belief system. Be it through fear or faith, nothing changes until something changes. This means that when entering recovery, you need to change your core belief system and amend your personal constitution to move in the right direction and to achieve sobriety.

Rigorous honesty is not passive—it is active. I call it glaring honesty. It is honesty in friendships with people and honesty when there's nobody else around. And you must get honest with God in the process. When I was drinking I used to throw empty beer bottles out the window of my truck. However, when I got sober and began to get honest deep down inside, I started watching what I did, and I found I couldn't litter anymore, even if nobody could see me doing it. It felt bad. I learned to be honest by being a companion to my own conscience. This didn't have anything to do with others because my dishonesty was an inside job.

Step 1 says: "*We admitted we were powerless over alcohol—that our lives had become unmanageable*". You can take the word alcohol and substitute whatever you want to put in there: food, pornography, drugs, or bad relationships. Some people probably even can put treatment programs in there. They keep going and going, and they don't get any better. They are powerless over treatment programs.

If you have an extra $30,000 and you are getting ready to go to another rehab center, give me the money! I'll take you to my house and you can stay there. I will feed you for 28 days and show you how to stay sober so you won't need to pay for recovery over and over. The 12 Steps and principles really are the only program that you need to achieve sobriety. You don't have to drink or use anymore and—most importantly—you don't have to travel any further down the pathway of destruction. You can end the suffering now, but if you want something that you've never had in your life before, you must do something that you have never done before to get it. This is not about adopting a process in which you will remain marginally sick and continue living in confusion. If you use the 12 Steps and principles correctly, you will be able to make a complete transformation and live a life that is happy, joyous, and free.

Many people who are active in addictions know The 12 Steps inside and out and have read volumes and volumes of recovery material. However, they have not done the required work and, as a result, they have not been able to stay sober. They remain in a cycle of failure because they refuse to take action, and it all starts with Step 1 and honesty. It's time to set down the gauntlet and say, "I want to rehabilitate my life, and I want to change so that I don't have to fail any longer, so that I don't have to go back to prison again or get arrested for another D.U.I."

I have recovered from alcoholism, and if this statement makes you nervous it's because you haven't read the whole story. Everybody wants to become a "grateful recovering alcoholic." That sounds really nice, but let me tell you what the truth is: We who have recovered from a hopeless state of addiction have found that in both mind and body things have changed. I am not saying that we are never tempted or that we don't have to stay vigilant in our sobriety, but or belief system and internal constitution has changed. Alcohol and drugs are no longer part of the daily equation. We are free from the daily battle, you can be too!

You are probably wondering and anxious to discover how and why with so much expert opinion to the contrary that we have gotten well again. My purpose in writing this book is to tell you exactly how I gained back my health and life and to share my experience, strength, and hope.

This brings me back to the first step of you journey and the fact that most addicts struggle with the concept of honesty. I will bet that every time you get a new resolve and decide that you are going to get honest, you say to yourself this time it will be different—but it never is. This may sound hopeless, but let me tell you something that will put it into perspective: The identification of dishonesty in your life is a sign that you are beginning to understand honesty, and you *are* starting to work on this principle.

You need to learn what dishonesty looks like in your life and how it has plagued you over the years. Many alcoholics and addicts have developed a lifestyle of lies, and many people in recovery still continue to skirt the truth. They go to meetings and fabricate tales that are not true, making things up so their stories sound better than the next person's. You may have lied so long that you are not even sure that you are lying!

Before I embraced sobriety I was in this category. I told lies to cover up lies. I would start telling little lies on Wednesday so that when Friday night rolled around and I told the big lie I could pull it off. Then I would tell more little lies all the way through Tuesday of the next week to cover up the big lie from the past Friday night. Did you ever live like that? I needed to remember what I said to get my stories straight, but most of the time I couldn't remember what it was that I said or to whom I said it. Sometimes I couldn't even remember where I was the past weekend, let alone who I told what.

The first cousin of dishonesty, and what gives dishonesty strength, is self centeredness. Addicts are selfish beyond belief because at the core of the disease is the quick fix. And when dishonesty and self centeredness are working in tandem you're in serious trouble. Caught in this trap, you are doomed to relapse. Moreover, you can't be partially honest. You must be thorough and completely truthful because as it has been proven if you don't get a hold of and build up an approach to living that requires painstaking honesty your life will not change.

Make no mistake: Honesty is the hinge pin of recovery. I don't care which program you are working or which recovery pathway you are traveling, it is essential for you to embrace this principle to break the cycle of addiction. As a result, you need to identify what it means to be rigorously honest. Below are some examples:

- **I will not cheat**—not at golf, not on my taxes.
- **I will not steal**—not even when a cashier gives back too much change.
- **I will not lie**. There are several types of lies:
  a. **Outright lies**—you knew it was a lie before you opened your mouth. "It's none of your business" falls into this category too.
  b. **Partial truths**—you withhold crucial information.
  c. **Enhanced truths**—you told the truth but then added information.
  d. **Shaded truths**—you use situational shading to improve your position depending on the audience/judge to make you look good.

Most people don't have a problem turning in a wallet if it is on the ground with some money and an I.D. in it. However, what if you left a meeting and there was an unmarked satchel leaning against your front tire with $50,000 in small bills? You might be inclined to say, "Thank you Jesus." However, you should not take it. It might not be Jesus, but "Benny the Hitman," and he's coming back with a gun looking for it!

Seriously, have you ever asked yourself if you were stealing from your boss? Every time you showed up at work with a hangover or still were high from the weekend, you were stealing. Consider some of the following examples of what honesty actually means:

- **You are trustworthy**. People would trust you to watch their animals when they go out of town.
- **You are truthful.** This also means you don't embellish the truth. The truth, the whole truth, and nothing but the truth.
- **You are sincere.** When you are genuine, what you see is what you get.
- **You are frank and open**. You say what you think.

- **You are straightforward**. You don't beat around the bush when giving explanations for your actions.

When you enter the recovery process, you need a trusted person to help you determine whether or not you are being honest. Why? Because we all have the capability to tell ourselves things and then believe them, when they are not true. I like to say, "Me is me problem. " I don't ever have to look far to find the enemy. I got up this morning, I looked in the mirror, and there he was.

If you are the problem, you cannot also be the solution without some help. You need to make sure that you are being held accountable by someone because you can move back into denial quickly. It can happen so fast you won't even know what happened. This is where a sponsor becomes indispensable. Find a sponsor early, use a sponsor often, and rely upon a sponsor heavily.

Denial is one of the biggest challenges you are likely to face as you begin Step 1. You may not be willing to acknowledge what is wrong with you. **DENIAL** means **Don't Even Notice I Am Lying.** You are not even aware that you are making things up! The unmanageability that resulted from your addiction needs to come into focus at Step 1. If you are in denial, then you really need to evaluate where you are at in your life to gain some clarity. If your address is a homeless shelter,, it's likely your life is unmanageable. If you are living in jail or prison or bouncing from rehab to rehab and you still are not sure if your life is unmanageable, how far down do you need to go to get the point? How often does something need to happen to you before something occurs to you? If you don't understand this, it will not be long before you start to justify the use of drugs and alcohol once you enter a recovery program.

To break this cycle, you must identify the root of the problem, and it's not necessarily connected to what alcohol or drugs did to you. That is easy to see. It sent you to jail or destroyed your marriage or maybe you got beat up in an alley trying to buy crack. Did any of these things ever happen to you? They probably did, and then you tried to convince yourself that you were a social drinker or user. Believe me, there are no social crack or heroin users out there.

This is the place where you have to break through the walls of denial and say there is something wrong, and it's not about what the substance did to you. You need to flip the coin over and see what it did for you and what it can do for you again. Denial also correlates to the level of pain you are experiencing. You can stay away from an addiction for a period of time, but if you don't actually do something to rehabilitate your life you will end up right back where you started sooner or later. Remember that when the pain in your recovery becomes greater than the pain that will result from the consequences of a relapse—relapse is inevitable.

You are not alone, unique or different. Almost all alcoholics and addicts feel like they are on the outside looking in and that they don't measure up. The loneliness and isolation that accompany this belief are unhealthy. Everyone is born with the need and desire for relationships. Think back to the time when you were born. You weren't afraid to ask for help. You cried, and after you did that a few times you realized you could yell and people would come. At about three days old you already realized that you could manipulate; you were a con artist already!

Maybe the following scenario sounds familiar. Early on in life you were open to relationships. As you got older, you lost the desire to interact and the ability to get close to others. It might have been a gradual shift or maybe it happened suddenly through a traumatic episode. It seemed that every time you got close to somebody or you got in a relationship the other person somehow hurt your feelings. You didn't know how to deal with it. Perhaps you grew up in a house that didn't allow you to discuss it. There was the proverbial pink elephant in the living room, but nobody was going to talk about it.

When you were out drinking or using year after year you tried relationships too, but they didn't work any better under the influence than they did sober. However, in that state you couldn't remember so you didn't care as much. Even as poor as the relationships were, the hurt still built up in your life, and it was not long before you recognized that the pain was there. Inevitably, you found yourself sitting in a bar or a crack house somewhere wondering what happened.

Don't you think you have dealt with problems like this long

enough? If you agree, then it's time to start the process and become honest with yourself and others. This is where the fellowship of 12 Step programs comes into play. The reason an alcoholic can identify with another alcoholic or a drug addict with another drug addict is because there is a common bond of experience. You both have been in the same pain. You have an understanding and you will need it when it comes time to give back to other people. You don't want to shut the door on the past, and you don't have to hide from it. Understand that it is there, and that you don't have to live in its wreckage. (By the way, the wreckage of your present is always rooted in the wreckage of your past.) All of the time you were active in your addiction was a wasteland, unless you utilize it going forward to help somebody else. Then it becomes your most valuable recovery tool.

You need to learn how to become honest to effectively reach out and touch other people and help turn the corner for somebody else. Honesty also is identifying that it's not about you at this point, it's about other people. For many years I tried to grasp the recovery process without being honest, and I tried to rehabilitate my life without the strength and power of a living, loving God. I failed. But the day I got honest, decided that I couldn't do this by myself, and cried out to God to intervene and help me —He did.

If you are an addict, honesty is of primary importance when asking for help. When I was getting sober and people were telling me things like "don't take the first drink," "it's the first drink that gets you drunk," and all the other clichés, I was lying to them when I said I understood. The reason I responded with a lie was because I didn't believe them, and I didn't think they would believe me if I told them the truth. I thought it might have been the 18th drink or the second day I was drinking that I got really drunk. I never connected the problem to the first drink.

I am not talking about moral failure here. I am talking about a physical addiction, a mental compulsion, and a spiritual bankruptcy that you have entered into. I don't know about you, but when I was getting sober I was not talking about an average problem. People were talking to me about my drinking—me giving up something that I loved. I wasn't a weekend warrior. I was a falling-down drunk, and I liked it. It was the thing that relieved my pain when nothing else could. It was magical and soothing. I would go to the bar and order up a big tall draft. The foam would spill over the side, and the jukebox would be playing my favorite song. I would have that drink and then the drink would have a drink. Then I had the third one, and the drink had me. I would get to that place where I had a glow, and all of the world's problems dissipated. Drinking was the love of my life.

People would say, "If you don't quit drinking I'm leaving," and I would say, "Good, I'll see you." I would give up anything so I could continue to drink. It was the only thing that ever made me feel normal until I became honest and found genuine recovery.

Do you remember the story of "Old Yeller?" It was about a boy who loved his dog. The dog was his best friend, it protected him, and it was his companion in life. But the dog got a disease. Old Yeller had become rabid, and he had to be put down. In the last scene of the movie, the little boy had his grandfather's shotgun. He was standing next to the corn crib where the dog was locked up. He knew if he didn't kill the dog, eventually the dog would kill him. He was caught in a dance of ambivalence, standing between two options: kill the dog and best friend that he loved or let it kill him.

At the end of my drinking I was standing in the same spot. I had to make a decision to put down my best friend—the bottle—or let it kill me. When I was at that point, I was not scared of what I would lose or the trouble I would have to face. I was afraid that I was going to die crazy. I was at a crossroads, and if you are reading this you likely have been in that position or you are in it now. You stand between two options, to live or die. **Choose life.**

A man went to heaven and he encountered St. Peter. St. Peter said, "Before we allow you to come in I need to ask you something. Did you do anything good in life?"

The man thought for a minute and he said, "Not that I can think of. I stayed to myself. I didn't bother with anybody, and nobody bothered me. I don't really think there is anything."

"Nothing?" St. Peter replied. "You never gave money to a poor man? You never volunteered at a charity? You never did anything good?"

"No, not a thing."

"You mean you never tithed or gave to the church? You never did anything for anybody," St. Peter asked in disbelief.

"I can't think of anything."

St. Peter replied, "I'm running out of time. You better come up with something."

"There is one thing."

St. Peter asked, "Well, what's that?"

He said, "I was coming out of this bar one night, I looked across the street, and there was a whole group of Hell's Angels. They had this old lady, and they were pushing her around. They had taken her purse and dumped it out. They were calling her names. So I ran right over into the middle of that group and I found the biggest, burliest biker. I slapped him in the face, and I said, "You leave her alone, or you are going to have to answer to me."

St. Peter said, "Well that's a really good thing. When did that happen?"

"About five minutes ago."

CHAPTER 2

HOPE

Until I embraced recovery, I tried to live by the words of the Simon & Garfunkel song I am a Rock. The lyrics go: "I am a rock, I am an island. And a rock feels no pain, and an island never cries." Although everyone starts out in this world as an infant with a need for relationships and care from others, when people get older and begin to encounter hurt, whether intentional or incidental, many times they withdraw and decide they don't need others in their lives because it causes pain. It's probably no surprise to you that most active addicts fall into this pattern.

As a kid in school, I always was the last one to get picked for any team in gym class. If there were an odd number of players, I was the kid who sat out. The message I received and the belief system that developed was that there is something wrong with me because you picked me last. The real truth was that I was terrible at sports and that is why the other kids didn't want me on their teams, but I didn't understand that at the time. I grew up on a dairy farm, and I was good at hauling hay and milking cows. I worked hard, and I was strong. But at school when I got around other people, I believed I didn't measure up. I always was on the outside looking in. I felt like this until the day I picked up my first beer. When I took that first drink I felt normal, perhaps for the first time in my life. I was free and happy, and I felt good at least for a little while.

I drank alcoholically from the beginning, always for effect—at any and every opportunity. And if the opportunity wasn't there, I created it. I drank alone, and that was just fine with me because I didn't need anybody. I didn't care; I wanted to keep people away. I grew up with a warped view of life. I was afraid of people and felt separate from my parents and the rest of the family. I wanted to be by myself and I lost all self esteem.

That changed when I started attending recovery meetings, and I learned that the repair of self esteem involves others. To build it back you must do "esteemable" things. When others compliment your actions you begin to heal emotionally. In the rooms, I watched people, heard their stories, and saw them laughing when they talked about what happened to them. At first it puzzled me. When I came in, I didn't have a sense of humor; nothing was funny. But after I developed a prayer life and acquired a feeling of safety in meetings, I began to see the humor. I started to see other people who had what I wanted and their examples instilled a new principle in my life: hope.

> **Step 2:** *Came to believe that a Power greater than ourselves could restore us to sanity.*

 PRINCIPLE: HOPE

Maybe you were given the impression by others that something was wrong with you, and you bought into the belief that they were correct. You became hopeless as a result. The truth is that you don't get low self esteem alone and you can't get out of it alone. The way you see yourself is based what you believe others think of you. In other words, I am what I think you think I am. Low self esteem comes from a lifetime of failed attempts at relationships. Each time you are hurt, a message registers in your subconscious that is based on perceptions rather than the reality of the situation. And each time you have a negative interchange it becomes increasingly difficult to relate to and trust others.

If you are just entering recovery, there's a good chance you have no hope and that you don't know where to turn. Everything is gone because you spent a big part of your life in self fulfillment, in the quick-fix mentality. You wanted to have it right now. You wanted instant relief. You wanted immediate happiness, and that is why you turned to alcohol and drugs. That's why you did all the things that you did, so you could feel good right now!

In every moment of your active addiction you reached into your future and stripped it of everything good to fill up today. You spent your future on instant gratification. Then one day you arrived at the point where you looked around and there was no future left. You had spent it all. There was nothing left to grab, no place to turn, and nowhere to go. You had ravaged your life so that you could feel good in the moment.

Now you need hope to carry on, and it is not some magical formula. Hope is what you see when you look into the face of another person in a recovery meeting and he or she seems happy, or when you enter a church and see somebody filled with peace and serenity. These individuals are not despairing like you. You can feel the difference, you can see the difference, and you can experience the positive emotions and energy emanating from them. When I first sobered up, I didn't get hope from what I heard. I got it from what I observed. I didn't believe anything people said. Their words were useless to me because all of my words were hollow and void. So when people talked to me, I didn't believe a single word that came from their mouths. But I did see people who came to meetings, shook hands, and hugged everybody. I watched them. I didn't know how to do those things, and I certainly didn't know how to relate, but it was something I wanted. I needed other people to share their experience, strength, and *hope* so I could get hope. I watched them being happy, and I gravitated toward them.

Hope is something you see that you don't have, and it activates an excitement and an expectation that you can attain it. It is when you look into the eyes of somebody who has recovered, or you look into the eyes of somebody who can build a relationship with God. I can assure you that if you see something desirable in someone else it is available to you. Remember the saying, "If you want what I have, you must do what I do."

If you encounter people who have something you want, they can become a power greater than yourself. It may be a mechanic who knows how to fix your broken car. It could be a doctor who can help cure a disease or a lawyer who can get you out of jail. Most importantly, if you have an addiction, other people in recovery can constitute a power greater than yourself when you start the journey into sobriety. God works through people. He puts them in your path, and that is the premise of a Power greater than you could restore you to a normal life.

I don't think that I have ever met anyone who suffers from addiction who has told me, "You know, when I was a child I said, 'When I grow up I want to be addicted to stuff.'" That is not a life goal. I'm sure the plan you had was to be successful in some way, but somehow your approach was faulty. So now it's time to get a new plan. However, if you develop a strategy that is designed around creating your own higher power it's not going to work. How can a power greater than you be created by you? You got yourself into this mess and you will not get yourself out of it without some help!

The first time I found hope was when I came face to face with another living person who was addicted to something who actually owned up to it and didn't come across as having all the answers. He said, "Well, I'm powerless, I don't know much, and I'm here working on myself." I liked that. For me, the higher power became human beings together in a recovery group. We could do together what I could not do by myself.

However, don't get tricked into thinking any group will function as your higher power if you are an addict. It's easy to find a church group that will pray for you and free you from the desire to drink. Then do you know what happens? You forget where you came from. I can say this because I have been a minister for more than 25 years, and I have seen it happen.

Someone will tell you something that sounds like this: "You used to be an alcoholic, but you're not an alcoholic anymore."

And you say to yourself, "Wow! That works for me. I don't have to go to meetings or do the step work or anything?"

You leave church, and you are feeling pretty good. You just got the silver bullet. And then you encounter the enemy. It's called you, and the problem is you have to ride home with you. You begin to talk to you about what they said about you. And what they said is you are no longer an alcoholic because the Lord has taken care of that.

You are driving along and then after awhile you say, "I never really thought I was an alcoholic. There were people telling me I was an alcoholic, but I don't think they knew what they were talking about anyway."

Later you say to yourself, "If I'm not an alcoholic I probably can stop and have just one drink on the way home to celebrate my new freedom."

You are off and running again, and then you blame the people at the church.

"Well, I got saved and it didn't work," you complain.

Yeah, it worked. You are just going to go to heaven drunk. Don't worry, I haven't lost my mind. The Bible says, No drunkard will see the kingdom of heaven. (I Corinthians 6:10) You have to understand that the kingdom of heaven is not where we go when we die. The kingdom of heaven is at hand. You have the kingdom right here, but you won't be able to see what's around you unless you sober up. There is a power greater than yourself that got you sober, but there is a process that is going to keep you sober.

Hope is half of faith. Faith is the substance of things hoped for and the evidence of things not seen. What is the substance of your hope? It is what you can see. There is a verse that says we walk by faith, not by sight. So faith is the higher level and sight is the lower level. The idea is I have hope when I see, and that is when faith actually starts. Hope is the natural realm, what you see, hear, smell, taste, or touch.

The most important words in this step are "could restore us." Let me focus on the word restore for just a minute. If I'm going to restore something, it means there was something in an original condition. You take an old motorcycle that's rusted and beat up and you restore it. You make it better than the original, and suddenly you realize that this motorcycle once was on a showroom floor. Then somebody bought it, rode it all over town, and crashed it into curbs and trees, neglected it and it got damaged in the process. Your life probably has a similar path of destruction but now you can be restored. The good news is at some point you must have had sanity if you are going to be restored to sanity.

Long before I picked up the drink I had problems. But I know there was a point in my life when I was normal. Some people believe they were born alcoholics or drug addicts. I think I drank too much, too long, too often and, as a result, I became addicted to alcohol. That's how I became an alcoholic. Did I have the characteristics of an addictive personality? Sure I did. But there was a time that I was not sick or insane, and that is the state to which I'm going to be restored.

Now I'm going to give you a little test. I want you to walk along with me mentally. Go back to when you were in the fifth grade. Think about where you lived at that time in your childhood. What color was your house? Where did you go to school? What was the name of the school? What was the building like? Was it wood, was it brick? I want you to recall your classroom. See if you can remember your teacher's name. Think about the cafeteria and lunch period. Can you remember what it smelled like? Remember the gymnasium and what it smelled like? You are at the end of the day. How did you get home from school? Did you ride your bicycle? Did somebody pick you up in a car? Did you walk?

You are at home, and you walk in the front door. What was the first thing you did? You probably went to the refrigerator. Did you turn on the TV? What was your favorite show? It's later in the evening, and now you are in your bedroom. It's time to go to bed. What did your bedroom furniture look like? What color was your room? You are in bed and you turn the light off. What was the last thing you think about before you go to sleep?

Now come back to the present and ask yourself: In your day as a fifth grader, how many times did you think about drinking or using drugs? You didn't. That's called sobriety. Where I walk today, I don't even think about a drink. I don't even consider a drink. It's no longer part of my psyche. It's no longer a part of what I do. At some point in my life, I had that dimension of sanity and sobriety returned to me.

You can achieve this goal too.

When I began to drink I stopped growing emotionally, so when I got sober I was only about 13 years old emotionally. I didn't know how to make friends or interface with men and women. However, by seeing other happy people in recovery I gained hope and I learned how to break the cycle of isolation that I had been in for most of my life. The insanity of being alone stopped when I could look into the eyes of others and connect with them. It began the process of trusting, and the walls of my crazy life began to tumble all around me. I started letting others in, and in the process I learned that the more I give out of my life the more I get back. But I cannot give something I don't have. The measure of what I give is determined by what I have. The measure of what I have is determined by what I receive, and the measure of what I receive is determined by what I give. It is a cycle.

I lived in a life of loneliness and isolation. While I am still a very private kind of person and I enjoy my time alone, today it is not isolation but solitude. I found out that there is a huge difference between isolation and solitude. Isolation is a dark cavern of desperation and solitude is a doorway to spiritual growth. The first place I found solitude was at meetings. They were a refuge, a quiet place where I broke free from all of the cares of life. I also found solitude when I went to church and I could sit for an hour or more in peace. The isolated state that I lived in during my active addiction was terrible, but solitude seemed to be a safe harbor where something good was going to happen. It was a reprieve from my problems for at least a short time.

Understanding the differences between isolation and solitude will help you break the cycle of loneliness in your life and find the hope you need to begin a full recovery from addiction. I have drawn the comparisons for you:

Isolation is a place of self indulgence; solitude is a place of self denial. When you are in isolation it is only about you, what you want, and how you feel. It is living a life of total self centeredness, and you hurt other people in the process. Solitude is being in a place of self denial, and it is where you begin to give back to other people. Your willingness to give to others is the only true proof that you have actually broken free from self centeredness.

Isolation is a place of silence; solitude is a place of communication. When you are in isolation it is totally silent except for the sound of your own thoughts, which are mostly negative, hopeless, and obsessive. Solitude is a place where you are in communication with others and with God, and your thoughts are productive and filled with insights and positive impressions.

Isolation is a place of running from something; solitude is running toward something. Are you escaping from family, responsibilities, bill collectors, the police, and even reality? Solitude is a place where you are not running from anyone or anything. You are running toward something, such as recovery or a spiritual life. You are heading in the direction where you are going to receive hope and help. You are moving toward your purpose and destiny.

Isolation is a place of draining; solitude is a place of filling. When you are in isolation it always drains you of energy. It will exhaust you of hope and vision. You become empty on the inside and the feeling of being alone and inappropriately unique are constant. When you move into solitude it's a place that fills you up. Spiritual strength, joy, peace, and the sense of belonging replace the emptiness.

Isolation is a place of turmoil; solitude is a place of peace. In addiction you are used to chaos and turmoil. You may even find in early recovery that you don't know how to function without disorder. Self destructive patterns of behavior emerge simply because you are drawn to the familiar confusion. When you get sober you suffer from terminal serenity! The newness of the peace you experience often is scary. Solitude replaces a sense of impending doom with an awareness that everything is going to be all right.

Isolation is a place of self will out of control; solitude is a place of self control. Self centeredness is the hub of addiction, and it breeds a state of isolation. It is all about you. Like one man said, "I'm not much, but I am all I think about." "If it feels good, do it" is the motto of today's society. Self control is the alignment of your self will with an outside standard. The place of solitude allows you to operate with guiding parameters in life.

Isolation is a place of inconsistency; solitude is a place of continuity. For many addicts, life seems like a series of disconnected episodes leading nowhere fast. Both feet firmly are planted in mid air! You are isolated from direction, purpose, and goals. Solitude is the state where realistic goals, plans, and visions are launched. Like the Bible verse says, "My people perish for lack of vision."

Isolation is a place where you play the role of Flesh Man; solitude is the land where Spiritual Man emerges as the leader. The addict is a physical person who wants everything—more alcohol, more drugs, more food, more sex, more excitement. Solitude is the land where your spirit becomes the guiding force. Learning to live through the direction of the spirit realms becomes an imperative when the Spirit of God becomes your guiding force.

If you take one drink or pick up a single drug, do you know what you really have lost?

Hope.

The first time you turn back to your addiction you immediately shut people out. You move back again to the dark world of isolation.

Isolation is a place of worry; solitude is a place of waiting. There is not much variance between the two. It's a matter of what you are seeking. Are you worried and expecting the worse to happen, or are you are waiting and expecting the best to happen? Both operate from the same premise of faith.

Isolation is a place of evil; solitude is a place of love. If you are caught in the cycle of addiction, the evil in this world is overwhelmingly apparent. Wrong thinking, wrong desires, and dominating fear overtake those couched in isolation. Unconditional love displaces all fear. The place of solitude you find when you enter into healthy, compassionate relationships drives away fear and the sense that the world is out to get you.

Isolation is a place of confusion; solitude is a place of wonder. If you are cut off from the rest of society nothing makes sense. Irrational thoughts replace mental clarity, and life is baffling and unfair. The mystery and color are gone from the world. Some people look into the night sky and are perplexed by what it all means. Others look into the heavens to see the stars and planets, and a wonderful sense of oneness and beauty captures them. Like a child, faith is inspired.

Isolation is a place of fear; solitude is a place of prayer. Fear is a tormenter. It will paralyze you and cause you to shut down into isolation and silence. Prayer is a great creator of solitude and peace. It opens up communication to the divine and draws power into lives that are hopeless.

Isolation is a place of weakness; solitude is a place of power. There is strength in numbers. Two in agreement are better than one standing alone. There is no encouragement alone, no interchange of thoughts, no strengthening of heart and character, no potency. Collectively we can do together what you can never do alone. Solitude gives you the power to create synergy and combine forces.

Isolation is a place where the devil is in charge; solitude is where God is in control. Have you ever felt like the devil is in charge? Unconditional surrender to a loving God is the only way to free your life from the grip of addiction. Surrender today, the sooner the better.

ISOLATION VS. SOLITUDE

Isolation	Solitude
Place of self indulgence	Place of self denial
Place of silence	Place of communication
Running from	Running toward
Draining	Filling
Turmoil	Peace
Self will	Self control
Inconsistency	Continuity
Flesh Man	Spiritual Man
Place of worry	Place of waiting
Place of evil	Place of love
Place of confusion	Place of wonder
Fear	Prayer
Weakness	Power
Devil in charge	God in control

Insanity is living in a pocket of isolation, and sanity returns when you learn to reside in the land of solitude. To do this you must be persistent in your inventory about relationships. Have you drifted away from meaningful interactions? Have you started isolating again? Have you stopped talking to people? Every relationship, either divine or human, requires the investment of time.

If you take one drink or pick up a single drug, do you know what you really have lost? Hope. The first time you turn back to your addiction you immediately shut people out. You move back again to the dark world of isolation. When you start feeling desperation, or you are down, you need to note you have move to aloneness. To come out of the isolation back to the safety of solitude, surround yourself with people who have hope and look into their eyes. Listen at meetings and if only one out of 10 people has something worthwhile to share grab onto it like a life preserver because hope floats.

Two men were at a bar having a shot and a beer,

and one man looked at the clock and said,

"It's really late. I'm in so much trouble."

His friend said, "You can't leave now. It's your turn to buy."

So the night continued on, and he went into the bathroom and

ran into another friend who pulled out some cocaine.

After that, he lost all track of time and it was three days before

he got home. When he finally walked in the door it was

Monday morning and his wife was fit to be tied.

She started yelling at him, and the berating lasted for hours.

Finally, she said, "What if you didn't see me for three days?"

He said, "Well I guess that would be alright."

So Tuesday came and went, and he didn't see his wife at all.

Wednesday passed, and not a sight of her. Thursday came and

went and he still didn't see his wife. Friday morning

arrived and his left eye was still the size of a baseball, but the

swelling had gone down just enough on his right eye so

that he got a glimpse of her.

CHAPTER 3
FAITH

I once operated a recovery program on the East Coast of Florida called Dayspring Worship and Recovery Center. It was fulfilling a life dream for me. The center was growing and it was having a positive impact on people's lives. However, not everyone involved wanted it to continue on the path I had charted, and there was friction and disagreement. The day came when the program shut down due to financial difficulties and problems with the board. A lot of things went awry because I had the wrong people helping to steer my ship. I thought we were all moving together with the same destination and objectives. I was wrong.

The best analogy I can make here is from the story of Jonah and the whale. To avoid doing God's will Jonah tried to flee across the sea in a boat. He was sleeping in the hull when terrible storm came up. Jonah awoke and knew that God had caused the storm in response to his flight from responsibility, so he owned up to being the deadweight (or the problem) and told the crew to throw him overboard. They complied, but instead of drowning Jonah was saved by God's mercy and swallowed by a giant fish (a whale). The fish returned him to land, and Jonah lived to tell the story and complete his mission for God.

Let's look at this from the ship owner's perspective. Something is going wrong and the ship is in peril. To save the vessel, all of the cargo must be thrown overboard. Keep in mind, he has to pay for everything that is discarded because he doesn't own it;

he is only the transporter. As the crew was throwing everything overboard, they discovered Jonah, and he identified himself as the primary reason the ship was going to sink. So they discarded him. I have never been quite sure if he really expected them to do it or if he had total faith in God's mercy to save him. Jonah was a man who was running away from God and everyone around him was paying for his lack of willingness. The ship owner didn't do anything wrong. The problem was the connection he had made with someone else.

I was the ship owner in this case, and it posed the question: Who is in the bottom of your ship and will that person or those people bring you down? After this happened, I became very cautious about connecting myself with others in business. This was a time in my life that I said, "Never again. I am never going to be a minister again. I am never going to help people again in a formal setting. I'm not running any more treatment programs. I am not doing any more service. I'm not praying for anybody else." I was done.

When the center shut down I was completely crushed. "Never again" became my mantra. However, then I realized that God, in His mercy, sustained me when I couldn't sustain myself. It was the God of my experience who cared about me. "A calm sea does not a good sailor make." Good sailors have been through some rough water, and they have learned how to respond. God has walked me through very difficult times, and He brought me out on the other side. As a result, I have faith, I operate in faith, and I live a life of faith. I also no longer associate with people who don't believe that God wants me to prosper. I associate where I am celebrated not tolerated. I have found my way back to ministry, building and running programs and ministering in church settings routinely.

> **Step 3:** *Made a decision to turn our will and lives over to the care of God, as we understood Him.*

PRINCIPLE: FAITH

I now tell anyone who is having difficulties in life to evaluate who is sailing onboard their ship. The one who is causing the most damage is the person who is not bothered by the storms. In the story of Jonah and the whale, when God created the life-threatening storm, Jonah was sleeping in the hull of the boat and wasn't at all bothered by the upheaval. Similarly, you might have somebody riding in your ship who you never considered might be dragging your life down. Perhaps you have a 23-year-old son at home. You can't pry him off the couch. He watches TV all day, eats all your food, refuses to get a job, and won't do anything but smoke dope while you are at work. He is in the bottom of your hull and you are wondering why you are in such dire financial straits? It's because there is somebody riding along on your dime. My advice is to ask your son one question: "Do you know how to swim?"

To make drastic changes in your life and eliminate the deadweight that is dragging down your attempts to break the cycle of addiction, you need faith. It is the principle of faith that is necessary to make the change. You cannot come to a place where you have a relationship, connection, or understanding with God until you acquire faith. And once you have that faith, you will develop a better understanding of your God. It's a reciprocal process. I believe the first round of faith is given to you when you are ready for recovery. You don't know how you ended up at a recovery meeting, but your life is falling apart, and you found yourself in that seat. Maybe you found yourself in the pew of a church, or you ended up somewhere where people were addressing the malady that afflicts you. You didn't have faith until you got there, but then suddenly you noticed where you were, and you began to believe you might have a chance. You have come to a place where you are now seeking God and become diligent about expressing the need for a relationship with Him.

The truth of the matter is that many people are not in that big of a hurry to locate God. Why? It's because if you locate God, you may discover that God is associated with some kind of parameters in your life that you have been trying to avoid for a very long time. You wanted to find God as long as God didn't require anything of you. You said to yourself, I'd like to find God as long as I am sure there aren't any rules that are going to mess up my fun. Or maybe you think, I would like to find God as long as I am positive I won't have to act like the nutty people who say they know God. Those are really scary folks. They bothered me and they were trying to force me to believe in God the way that they believe in God. And they even knocked on my door early on a Saturday morning when I was recovering from a hard night at the bar. You know I'm not very receptive to hearing about God when I have a hangover and I only had two hours of sleep.

When I was beginning to work the process of recovery as it pertains to faith, God didn't seem too far away and I discovered something: He has never forced Himself upon me. Every time that I had a little conviction about God, I chose to drink instead of follow my conviction, God never did anything about it. He never slapped a drink out of my hand. God will not come and jerk a crack pipe out of your mouth. God knows about it, but He will not stop you from doing it. However, the crack man might if you run out of money!

In recovery I discovered something about God. He was not trying to impose Himself upon me, but He wanted me to know that He was available. When I was growing up, there were only four television channels. There wasn't much of a selection, and one of the things that used to come on and bother me was Billy Graham. Not because I had anything personal against him (I think he is a wonderful man), but because he would take up a whole channel, usually for a couple of hours and I would miss out on whatever show might have taken its place!

That was a long time ago, and now it is clear to me one thing that Billy Graham had to offer. He was telling people that there is a God out there and you can access Him directly. And then he'd suggest a way to do this step. Of course, he didn't call it a step, but he said there was an opportunity for you to actually enter into some type of relationship with God on your own, even if you were at home watching TV. As a result, millions of people made their decisions to connect with God while they were listening to his show.

As a part of this process, Graham explained a concept of God so that people would have a better understanding when making a decision to establish contact. Similarly, when it comes time for Step 3 you need an understanding of God before surrendering your will over to His care. You are not going to give your life over to something you do not grasp. The process becomes much easier when you have awareness that God loves you. He is not mad at you. God is not out to get you and punish you. He loves you. God cares about your life and He can empower you to become successful.

This is a process; you can make a decision and then change your mind. Some people say they turned it over and then took it back, and then turned it over and took it back again. Basically what they are saying is that they connected with God, learned there were rules, decided they didn't like them, and then started doing their own thing again. Then the pain got so great that they asked God to help once more. Again, God showed them the things they were going to have to do and they decided it was not for them, so they went back out into their addictions. A person in this pattern did not turn their will and life over to God. He or she made a decision to see if they could get out of the fire long enough to cool down.

Face it: **You didn't find the recovery process because you saw the light. You found recovery because you felt the heat!** Your mother was mad and you were sleeping on the couch, or maybe in the garage. The heat was on. Your boss said one more time and you are out of here. Maybe it was a judge, and he just explained that you got a D.U.I. for the fourth time and you are going to prison.

If you keep walking into the same messes and you don't care what anybody else says, you will end up in such a quagmire that you have to ask for help. In this case, you are not coming to God by choice. You are looking for a quick fix, a temporary answer to a persistent, ongoing problem. Maybe in the past you believed the "God solution" seemed long and drawn out because you were forced to go to church and the formality of the experience made God boring. Now you think it's going to be sobriety by boredom. God will bore you so much that you no longer will want to drink or use drugs.

If you are in this type of situation, one in which you need help but you are rejecting God, you are hearing two voices. One is compelling, drawing you toward God and the other is pushing you to stay in your addiction to numb the pain. The open invitation to try to find a relationship with God is on one side and the draw of your addiction is on the other side. You are standing between the two trying to figure out which way to go. Are you going to die in your addiction, or is something going to happen that is going to turn you around?

You don't have to wonder about this anymore. You can break free from the trap of addiction. God is available and you can tap into His power, which is greater than you and your addiction. I have heard the explanations of how to do this become so complicated that I have to move away from the explainers. Some are praying to a tree or a light post or an alligator. If you use the alligator one don't bow your head or close your eyes. The pathway of the Christian's makes the process so simple. Identify God by name, they call Him Jesus. Ask Him by name to help you; pretty simple process. You can connect with that power and a church is not required to do it. God is not worried because you haven't made it to the right meeting place. He can find you wherever you are at.

You have an opportunity to turn your will and life over to the care of God. However, it isstill your will and your life and you have to take responsibility for them. I'm sure you would like to turn it all over and forget about it, but turning it over to God without taking responsibility produces people who are not grounded. You can't just abandon life's responsibilities because you have found God. As a matter of fact, He wants to empower you to have success in your life. God has not designed you for failure; so you can continue in the pathway of addiction and destruction. What's more, He didn't make a plan for you to fail once you get sober due to neglect and laziness.

I don't believe that God makes mistakes. I don't think He can. At one time or another, you probably have thought that perhaps God made a mistake with you. You looked in the mirror and you didn't like what you saw, but he didn't make an error in your physical appearance. And He didn't make a mistake in your personality; it just may not be developed yet. I believe that many addicted people have undeveloped personalities. I have watched people free themselves from alcohol and drugs and then witnessed them blossom into their full being.

Most people living with addictions have the following three character traits before entering into recovery:

Extreme rebellion, which produces indifference or intolerance.
Fierce independence, which creates reliance on their own ability.
Radical self centeredness, which means I want what I want when I want it.

It's interesting to note that most addicts are concerned with image. It's all about your image and how people perceive you, and how you perceive people perceiving you. In other words, you are what you believe other people believe about you. Some men are really scared so they put on a tough guy exterior. Some women are really wounded and don't know love so they become promiscuous and start connecting with any man who will give them the time of day. Indeed, there are different ways you can mask your insecurities and how you have been damaged in life, but they will begin to fade away when you understand that God has a purpose for you and you develop faith. If you tap into it, His will and His purpose will come into connection with your will and your purpose.

In this regard, I want to talk to you about the God of my experience, which explains the God of my understanding.

In 1980, I prayed and asked God to intervene in my life. I could not set down alcohol and drugs even for a short period of time. Then the God of my experience came and rescued me. Now that I have been sober for more than three decades, I have experienced God in every way conceivable, and it has been amazing. The God of my experience is not mad at me. He has a plan for my life and I have a plan for my life as a result of understanding that. Do you have a plan for your life? Do you have a plan for the next 90 days? Do you have a plan for the next year? Did you set some goals at the beginning of this year? If you didn't then you don't love yourself as much as God loves you. Here are two examples of how I've experienced His love:

The God of my experience helps me when I make really bad choices, particularly when it comes to people. I lacked the capability to have a healthy partnership with another human being on any level until I recovered from addiction. Can you relate to that? I just didn't connect with people. It wasn't relationships that were a problem, it was people. I didn't like people. I didn't have appropriate boundaries. I didn't have a good understanding of communication. I didn't have any benchmarks to gauge my relationships with other people except for my past relationships, and most of my experiences were bad! However, my relationships didn't always fail because of what I did. Quite often things didn't work out because the people connecting with me were not right for my path. God showed me that when you start doing the right things for the right reasons, the wrong people and the wrong things will exit your life. God will break you out of chaos and He will put people around you who will stand with you, tell you that they love you and care about you, and step up to the plate.

The God of my experience never misses a meeting, and I've been to more than 12,000. I heard from God early in my recovery and He's been at every meeting since. His communication to me was clear then and it still is now. I felt His love, presence, power, and forgiveness. I felt freedom from the compulsion to drink and use drugs. He did for me what I could not do for myself. I discovered that I could hear the voice of God, and now I listen to it every day. He's sending messages to me so that I can align my will with His will. Overall, the God of my experience has intervened in so many ways. He has healed me from being broken, crushed, despondent, and despaired. He also has relieved me from being an angry man who was afraid of everything.

Now I want to switch gears and address the relationship between spirituality and morality as it pertains to the principle of faith. You may have an abundance of spiritual concepts lodged in your head and wholeheartedly believe you are a spiritual person, but if you are stealing money from someone you are not on the right path. There is a moral requirement when you acquire faith and turn your will and your life over to God. I'm not going to dictate what your moral standards should be or what your conscious should sound like, but I want you to know that when you connect with God your conscious becomes clear. Suddenly you know what is right and what is wrong. You make the decision to abide by a moral compass and trust God. Your choices are not dictated by alcohol or drugs. They are not made by your therapist or your family or by a police officer, a boss, or a pastor for that matter. You have made a decision to follow God's will, and it is a personal decision. This process requires faith.

Faith is an unseen element because divine intervention is involved. According to Hebrews 11:1, "Faith is the substance of things for which we hope, the evidence of things not seen." Remember that the principle of hope is based on sight. Faith is stronger, because it connects the unseen world with the seen world. Faith is made up of two parts, the substance of hope and the evidence of the unseen, which is the spirit realm. It would look like this in a formula:

$$SH + EU = F$$

$$\text{THE SUBSTANCE OF HOPE} + \text{EVIDENCE OF THE UNSEEN} = \text{FAITH}$$

When the evidence of the unseen is coupled with the substance of hope it produces a belief that something good will happen. This is called faith, and you must develop your own individual relationship with God to realize it. You need to find your own way to connect with the God of your understanding, and it is a unique expression of your personality and beliefs. I think this is similar to the way children build bonds with their parents, and my own personal experience is a perfect example.

I have three sons, and I raised them by myself most of my adult life. When my boys were the ages of five, two, and one I found that they each had a unique way of approaching me. For many years there wasn't a single night that went by during which I slept uninterrupted. In the middle of the night I would hear my oldest son get up and he would come in next to my bed and bump it over and over and say, "Dad you awake?"

"Yeah David, I'm awake."

"Dad, I'm going to get a drink."

"OK David," I would say.

Then I would hear him walk down to the kitchen and rustle around getting a drink. Then he would come back and I'd be just about asleep. He would come to the side of the bed again and start bumping it and say, "Dad you awake?"

"Yes David, I'm awake."

"Dad, I'm going back to bed now."

"Goodnight David."

"Goodnight Dad."

My second son Stephen would wake up in the middle of the night and sit up in his bed calling out, "Dad, Dad, DAD, DAAAD!"

He would call Dad until I would say, "What is it Stephen?"

"Would you get me a drink of water?"

"OK," I would respond, and I'd get up and I would get him a drink of water. Then I would tuck him back in.

"I love you Stephen."

"I love you Dad."

"Goodnight Stephen."

"Goodnight Dad."

Then I would go back and crawl into bed.

My youngest son Andy was a little different than the other two. I would hear footsteps coming. He would hit that floor running and come down the hallway. He would jump up on the bed and wrap his arms around my head until I could hardly breathe and he would say, "I love you DADDY!"

"What do you need, a drink of water?"

"Yeah Daddy I need a drink of water."

I would get him a drink of water, and then I would carry him back to bed.

"Goodnight Andy. I love you."

"I love you Dad."

"Goodnight Andy."

"Goodnight Dad."

One night, after I was out late and lying in bed exhausted, the whole process started into motion again. However, this time when I finally crawled back under the sheets at 3:00 am I had somewhat of an epiphany. Having dealt with each of my sons and just as I was ready to close my eyes, I heard God speak to me, and I said, "Not you too!"

What God said to me was profound: "You know how your boys are? That's the way my children are. Some of my kids go out and do what they are going to do, and then they tell me when they are done. Some of my children sit in the middle of their dilemmas and cry until I come and rescue them; and I always come and rescue them. Some of my children just run and *Your opinion of God doesn't change God* jump up in my lap and tell me how much they love me, and they don't even have to ask for what they need. David, your children are a good example of how I have relationships with my children; each one in his or her own way."

Each one of my boys had their own approach and unique way of communicating, but it didn't change me as their father. I loved them all equally and I still do. The same is true of God. I don't know what your approach is and it does not matter, as long as you develop faith, find a relationship with God, and then connect with Him. **Your opinion of God doesn't change God.** Your approach and your ideas don't change God. Don't wait until you have been faltering year after year in recovery programs to find faith and build a bond. Pray, pursue, and partake of His love now. Remember that a fool does at the end what a wise man does in the beginning.

This good old boy had a new four-wheel-drive pickup truck. He was out one night, and he lit up through town going about 100 miles per hour. A rookie cop pulled out behind him, chased him down, and finally pulled him over. The officer came up and said, "Do you have your driver's license?"

"I don't have a driver's license."

"Well what about the registration for this truck?"

"Well," he said, "I don't have a registration for the truck."

"Can I look in the glove box?"

"You can't go looking in the glove box," he replied.

And the officer said, "Well why not?"

"Because there are drugs in the glove box."

"Get out of the truck!"

"I am not going to open the door because you might see the loaded handgun underneath the seat."

So the officer opens the door, pulls the guy out, and he places him up against the truck.

"Don't go lifting the tarp up off the back of the bed," he said. "There is a dead body under there."

So the officer puts him in the police car. Then another cruiser arrives, and a backup officer gets out and asks what's going on. The rookie tells him the driver has no license, no registration, drugs in the glove box, a gun under seat, and a dead body in the bed of the truck. The second police officer went over and spoke to the guy.

"Well what's going on here?"

"I don't know," he replied.

The officer said, "I understand you are driving without a license."

"I've got a license in my wallet if you want to check."

"What about a registration?"

"Yeah, there is one in the glove box."

"Didn't you tell the other officer there are drugs in there?"

"There aren't any drugs in there, but you can look if you like."

"What about the handgun underneath the seat."

He replied, "There is no handgun underneath the seat, but you are free to take a look."

"Well, what about the dead body in the back of this truck?"

"You mean that other officer told you that! What a liar. There is no dead body. He probably told you I was driving 100 miles an hour, too."

CHAPTER 4
COURAGE

Once I had spent some time in recovery, I mustered the courage to head to Nashville, Tennessee to become a song writer. Like many people who have been sober for a few years, I developed a burning desire to follow a dream. As a result, I found myself on Music Row working out of a flop house with hundreds of other wannabe writers. Next to the boarding house was a publishing company with 300 staff writers, and it was not the only professional music company on "16th Avenue". Everyday there were writers and musicians sitting around playing their latest songs and discussing how the lyrics they just wrote would be the next big hit, if only they could get a big time producer to listen. I was no different, and I was sure I had the next big hit if only…

One day I ran into a producer at a recovery meeting. It was a chance meeting that I immediately attributed to God's arrangement. I was sure this was it! I went to his studio, a rather elaborate setting, and we exchanged small talk. He asked me to play something for him, and I willingly obliged. More small talk and I went on my way. Then I waited for the call to come, but it never did. Days later I had an epiphany: There wasn't an agent looking for my No. 1 hit song, and nobody was likely to come and hire me to write a song when there were 300 professionals working next door. The big guys had lots of money, lots of songs, and lots of opportunity. I just wasn't a part of their plan, nor was I likely to be in the future.

There are times that we can live in the obvious, at least what is obvious to others, and not see the reality of the situation for ourselves. However, as a result of the work I had done in recovery and my experience with the principles, I was able to inventory my situation in

Nashville and I saved myself from the disaster of becoming another frustrated, unemployed song writer. By the way - - - I still have a number one best seller song - - - in case you wanted to know!

Step 4: *Made a searching and fearless moral inventory of ourselves.*

PRINCIPLE: COURAGE

If you are ready to face your life head on, it is time for the inventory process. During this critical juncture in recovery, much of what you have hidden from yourself about your personality, character defects, and moral values—both good and bad—will become apparent. Until now, you probably have believed that your life is based on random occurrence. You are just the victim of chance or bad luck. The truth is that your circumstances are the result of cause and effect. You reap what you sow, and you have been harvesting from all of the bad seeds you have planted in your past. However, this cycle will change if you put down the drugs and/or alcohol and let go of any other addictive behaviors that are bringing you down; face reality; and find the obvious.

So are you prepared to make a searching and fearless moral inventory of yourself? It's one of the most difficult steps in recovery, but the most necessary to make a permanent change. The primary principle associated with Step 4 is courage. It will require *great courage* to be totally honest with yourself about your life. But trust me, it will be worth it!

You need to note that this step doesn't say immoral inventory. It says a moral inventory. When most people first look at this process they immediately say: "I need to write down all the bad things I have ever done." While you do have to list all of the negative behaviors from your past, that is not the end of the inventory. This is a comprehensive look at your life in its entirety, not just one fragment of it that contains all of the bad things you did. Principles 1 through 3 introduce you to the concept of living a life based on spirituality, and principle 4 is the point at which applying that spirituality becomes imperative.

A moral inventory implies that there is a moral standard. Hence, this inventory is both moral and spiritual. It is impossible to live life on a spiritual plane without a moral standard. They are inseparable. You are not living spiritually when you are still stealing, lying or hurting others either physically or emotionally.

This is the place where you need to understand that the root causes of your disease are those things you hold in secret. Secrecy is a large component of addiction. Addiction is a disease; a "dis-ease" is a disorder. There is something physically wrong with people who develop addictions. Moreover, there is something mentally and emotionally impacting the situation as well. Many addicts are obsessive/compulsive in nature. There usually is some form of depression, or there are highs and lows where one minute you are way up on the top of the world, and then you fall off and land down into a gutter. It's all a part of the disease.

Addiction is a disorder in which you become spiritually bankrupt and fearful. Immoral behaviors are involved, but they are more a by-product of the disease than a cause. It is a downward spiral with fear feeding every part of your life. I can assure you that the primary reason you have not taken an inventory is because of fear. You say to yourself: *I am afraid of what I might find. I am afraid of what I might run into. I'm afraid of what I might learn in this whole process. I am afraid of what I might find out about myself. I am afraid of what I might find out about my life.*

For the purpose of your inventory, I have broken fear into four main types. Clearly, this is not designed to be an exhaustive study of fear, but some thoughts to assist you in seeing your own fears.

Healthy fear. This fear is something you need to survive. A man with a gun pointed at you should elicit fear. Looking both ways before crossing the road because you might get hit by a car also is a healthy fear. Healthy fear will keep you alive. It produces a normal, reactionary response.

Intermittent fear. This fear occurs at intervals in life. It happens when a hurricane is looming off the coast and you live in its path at the beach. An unexpected sickness will bring on intermittent fear. It produces a planned response. You simply take the appropriate plan of action and eventually overcome the fear.

Exaggerated fear. Examples in this category include fear of elevators, heights, and other phobias. The fear is real and the situation that produces it also is real; however, the response is based on a distortion of reality. This produces an obsessive, exaggerated response.

Abnormal fear. This is a false fear that is not based on reality, but on something that doesn't exist. This is being afraid of the unknown. Fear of the dark is a good example of abnormal fear, which produces an overactive response or panic. Your decisions and your thought processes are based on your experience. As an addict, most of your experience has been bad, so consequently your decisions and your thought processes are bad. Bad experiences produce bad decisions, which produce more bad experiences. It is a vicious cycle that results in abnormal fear.

In analyzing fear, remember that fact and truth are not the same thing, just as experiences and meanings are not identical. The experiences you have may be different than the meanings you attach to them. In other words, meaning is the interpretation of your experience, and this is a key point in your inventory. It's not what you experienced so much as what you perceived you experienced. And most likely your perception was and still is effected by low self esteem, low self worth, low self image, as well as the memories of all of your failures and shortcomings.

I was no exception to the rule, and when it came time for me to take the Step 4 inventory I began to operate in fear that was fed by my perceptions. Here's an example of how this type of warped discernment works. I went back to my hometown in western New York shortly after I sobered up. I left home when I was 17, and I had not been back since. Before I made the trip, I remembered what my house and my old school looked like, but when I arrived they were nothing like I remembered! The school didn't look big, but it seemed huge in my mind. Then there was the little house that I grew up in. I thought I lived in a big fancy farmhouse, but it was a shack. It wasn't anything glamorous, and it had a wood stove. Then suddenly it all flashed back to me: I grew up chopping wood. My perceptions of where I grew up were entirely wrong, and if my observations of my physical surroundings were off, then certainly I needed to consider that my perceptions of actual experiences with people during that time were not accurate as well.

When I entered recovery, most of my memories were what I call creative history. My story was never quite the same each time I told it. It was interesting when I first started out because most of it was fantasy. I told the people at meetings about all these crazy things that I did. (The weirder you were, the better they liked you, or so I thought.) And then one day my sponsor pointed out that my story was probably bad enough as a standalone. I didn't need to add anything to it. The embellishments finally stopped after I did the fourth step inventory and became honest and truthful about my life.

People often ask me, "Am I supposed to be working on my inventory?"

"Well, I don't know for sure," I respond. "But I suppose if your asking the question then the answer is yes."

If you feel like you are supposed to be working on your inventory then work on your inventory! Don't get caught in the paralysis of analysis. You don't need to make it a complicated decision. You'll feel a shift when it's time to begin to sift through your life and look at everything. I didn't get permission from my sponsor to do inventory. I discovered on my own that I was in the season where all the memories from the years of my drinking were coming to the surface. I would be sitting at meetings, people would say things, that would activate thoughts, and I felt the need to write those thoughts down. So I began to take a searching and fearless look at my life without even consciously making the decision.

At the point when you begin the process you are entering into a vision for your recovery, and you need to have a singular focus. The opposite of vision is division. Vision says that I can go forward, and division—or lack of singular purpose—says that I'm not ready. In the case of the latter, part of you says "I want to take an inventory," and the other part says "I am afraid." Or one side of you says "I need to take an inventory," and the other says "I want to go out and drink or use drugs."

After fear, the second thing that will keep you from starting your life review is procrastination. You have become entrenched in the mindset that if it feels good, it must be right. The hard look at your life does not feel good, so you don't want to do it. When you get up in the morning you need to recognize where the enemy lives, and it's inside you. You need to look in the mirror. You need to talk to yourself or you will become trapped in your old ways of thinking. You need to understand that if it feels good it doesn't necessarily mean that it is right.

Courage comes from knowing what to expect, so it's time to discuss exactly what you should address as you begin the inventory process and enter into this amazing part of your journey. There are seven specific areas that I suggest you outline: season, size, sound, stoppages, shortfalls, strengths, and spiritual condition.

Season. Your life has seasons, but they are not determined by a calendar, they are determined by purpose. If you ever lived in snow country you probably know what I'm talking about. You would look at the calendar and realize it was the first day of spring, but when you looked out the window there was a blizzard going on. The calendar changed, but the weather outside did not match it. So remember when you come into the season of the inventory, it's not about time. Maybe you are in a season during which you have no money, no car, and you have debts outstanding to several people. You need to straighten this mess out. Maybe you are in a season of bad relationships and you will not be ready for another one until you get through it. Try to identify what season you are in. Do this for different aspects of your life.

Size. Are you "right sized" for your life? This is a very important part of your inventory. When I first entered recovery I used to stretch the truth about my sobriety date. Have you ever done that? It's more than 30 days, so I'm in my first six months. I'm in early sobriety. I'd get up to one year and receive a medallion and somebody would ask me, "How long do you have?" I would reply, "I'm working on my second year." I led them to believe that I was a lot closer to year number two than I was to year number one. I had to exaggerate. As another example, I hadn't completed my education and I had no job skills, but I made some up. I made everyone believe that I was something that I wasn't. I was "wrong sized."

If you are broken and damaged, you're broken and damaged. Just stop pretending. When I was four years sober I was ready to lose my house, but everybody believed I was rich. Because of how I felt about myself and other people's opinions, I couldn't ask anyone for help. Now how ignorant is that? Look at situations in your life that are similar to this when you are making an inventory.

Sound. What does your recovery sound like? Maybe you are new in the rooms and every place you go you hear people telling you, "Don't drink and go to meetings." Maybe a month or two later everyone is saying, "Get a sponsor. Why haven't you found a sponsor?" It's important to reach a place where you can inventory the sound of your recovery at any given time. Are you hearing, "Work the steps?" God is trying to deliver messages to you, and He will talk to you through the voices of other people in recovery. Listen closely and heed God's words because if you lose the sound of your recovery, the sound of your addiction will return. You probably have heard it: "Just one wouldn't hurt, no one will know, you're not hurting anyone else…"

Stoppages. What causes you to stop when you are doing your inventory? You need to identify the walls that block you. Maybe it's legal matters that you never addressed, abuses that you perpetrated against somebody else, or family that you let down. If you write these things down it will help you get through the humps. I've found that the number one thing that will stop you is not wanting to be embarrassed, particularity if you owe people money.

Shortfalls. You need to identify where you come up short. Maybe your inventory is not going forward because you don't know how to write very well. Your ability to read and write has been impaired because you have never had the opportunity to learn. Let me tell you something, this doesn't mean that you are ignorant. It just means that you have not yet learned these skills yet. You need to plan to overcome any challenges that will keep you from continuing on in the inventory process. You might consider asking your sponsor to help you write down your inventory or use a tape or digital recorder to help in the process.

Strengths. You must uncover and learn about your positive qualities. God wants you to surrender your weaknesses, but He also wants you to surrender your strengths. You can never become everything that God wants you to become, regardless of how long you have been sober, if you refuse to share with Him the things that make you strong. I know what my strengths are today, and I lean into them. And I stopped apologizing for the gifts that God gave me. You can do this too!

Spiritual condition. Your inventory is the best place to learn how to measure your spiritual condition. In recovery, you are granted a daily grace based on this dimension of life, so you need to measure what creates spiritual fitness for you. You need to measure your prayer life and the time that you spend studying things that are inspirational. Maybe you need to look at the meetings you attend and the connection that you have with a sponsor—a sponsor who actually knows God. If your sponsor doesn't believe in God, then I don't believe you have a true sponsor. I wouldn't follow somebody who doesn't believe in God through a process designed to connect you in a relationship with God.

If faith is the opposite of fear, then courage is the antidote for fear. If you are afraid to do something, do it afraid. You take courage. You need to have an attitude that says, I'm going to face this thing, and I'm going to walk into it.

Today, I'm not afraid of anything. I'm not scared of people. Before I recovered, I was terrified of people, and I was afraid to speak in front of anyone. I would have panic attacks at meetings when everyone would take turns sharing by going around the room. All I would be thinking about was what I was going to say when it was my turn. I was so wrapped up in myself that I would say something stupid. Then after I said it, nobody laughed and everybody looked at me funny. I would be embarrassed, and they moved on quickly. I would spend the rest of the meeting thinking about whatever it was that I said that was so stupid. Early on in sobriety I was living in fear, and I had to fake courage. To do this, I had to remember that I couldn't believe everything I thought because many times it just was not true.

A searching and fearless moral inventory means that you need to look at whatever it is no matter how scared you are. And to get from fear to faith, you have to use the bridge of courage. You learned some about faith and now you are at the place where the rubber meets the road and you hit reality. To help you cross that bridge, here are the seven things that define courage:

1. **Courage is an active decision** to respond in a productive way to fear.

2. **Courage is not backing down** when you feel like running.

3. **Courage is getting up just one more time** than you have been knocked down.

4. **Courage is not surrendering** when you feel hopeless.

5. **Courage is doing something in spite of the fears**, not the absence of fear in your life.

6. **Courage is walking into fear.**

7. **Courage is taking action** in the face of danger, calamity, or discouragement.

Many people have problems understanding how to do their inventory, and I was no exception. It was confusing. I tried to figure it out, but I just couldn't connect the dots. Indeed, there are different ways to undertake this process, so I want to share another approach and some great advice I received my first time out of the gate. When I was getting ready to start my inventory, this old guy sat down right across from me at a meeting. He just looked at me and said, "So I guess you are having trouble doing your inventory." He hit it squarely on the head for offering unsolicited information. "You don't know when to start it. You probably don't know if you're supposed to begin when you had your first memory in life, when you reached puberty, or when you had your first drink."

He said not to start at some illusive point that I didn't really know. "You only have today, so start with today," he explained. "Yesterday is gone, tomorrow is not here. Yesterday is a cancelled check, and tomorrow is a promissory note. Today is all you have, so spend it wisely. What's the No. 1 thing you need to work on right now? Maybe fear."

I thought somebody was holding cue cards for him.

"Write down everything you can think of that makes you afraid today, and then back up to yesterday," he said. Then do the same thing with last month, and then go through your life. Finally, write down the things that scare you about your future, and then come back to today. You will have inventoried all of the fears that you have had in your entire life and you will end up on today because today's all you've got."

It made a lot of sense to me, and I hope it helps provide you with another way to jump into this step. Once you understand this concept you can move on to other emotions, such as anger, and handle them the same way. Remember that depression is anger without enthusiasm, and usually you are angry at yourself!

In closing here's how this process helped to change my life for the better. During my inventory, I went all the way back in my life to my first memory. Along the way, I found I was having trouble with relationships, and I had to get a professional counselor to help me sort it out. It became apparent that my picker was broken when it came to women!

So I went back and I found that at the beginning of my life there was a negative message about relationships. And when something like this happens it imprints in your brain's neural pathways, and it can impact you for the rest of your life. I was just a toddler sitting on the bed and my dad was standing on one side and my mom was standing on the other, and they were screaming at one another. And it put a message in my head that relationships are all about screaming and yelling. When I discovered this, I wept.

The clarity allowed me to change what I believed about intimate relationships. The result was I stopped picking the wrong partners; women who didn't have complementary personalities and values. As a result, I stopped the pattern of continuous fighting and failing in my relationships.

When you do your inventory properly, you can travel through time mentally and go back to any place in your life to discover the root causes of your major life problems and unacceptable behaviors. The good news is that you absolutely can correct them. I can assure you that God will remove your emotional discomforts if you embrace the courage to complete a absolute, systematic inventory of your years. Everything that you can feel, God can heal.

There was a drunk guy walking down the street,
and he was looking for some money. He saw a guy
painting
a house, so he stopped and asked,
"Hey, do you need some help?"
"Do you know how to paint?" the man asked.
"Yeah, I can paint."
"Alright, get that bucket of paint and the brush
and go around in the back and paint the porch."
So the drunk took the bucket and brush and he went
behind the house. About half an hour later
he came out with
paint all over his hands and on his clothes, and the paint
bucket was empty.
"You can't be finished already!"
"Oh yeah I am," the drunk said. "I'm finished.
But I want you to know that's not a Porsche,

that's a BMW."

CHAPTER 5

INTEGRITY

During my tenure as the director of large facility that helped homeless people, I had regular confrontations with an older alcoholic woman who used to hang out on the back porch of the building. She was living on the streets, dirty and disheveled, and she was fond of threatening me. Whenever I saw her she would shake her fist and shout, "You shouldn't be out here talking to me and telling me what to do." "I'm gonna cut your head off and send you to see Jesus!"

Finally, one day I was walking out back and there she was looking at me sternly and I was expecting another verbal attack. But instead she said, "Dr. Sutton I want some help. Can you help me?"

I said, "Come on, let's go."

I took her by the hand and I walked her in the building. All the staff looked at me as if I had gone crazy, Some people said, "Why are you bringing her in?" They knew her.

I said, "She wants help, so let's help her."

We enrolled her into the program that night. It was a couple of months before she was stable enough to participate in classes, but we got her cleaned up and we started learning some things about her. She actually had ability and willingness. She went all the way through the program and graduated. We discovered during the process that she had a master's degree in mathematics. She was incredibly intelligent and witty. She had family in North Carolina. She had people who cared about her. It was remarkable.

Even more amazing was that she had killed a man and had

served time in prison for murder. When she was finally released, she never figured out how to assimilate back into society and she was stuck in a pattern of defeat and humiliation. (Unfortunately, this is the case with most people coming out of incarceration and/ or the prison of addiction.) However, once she opened up about her past, addressed it, accepted it herself, and then made a decision to share it with others and God, she was able to move past her difficulties and start a new life. She found integrity.

When she finally made it through the fire, I looked at her one day and said jokingly, "I saw your record. If I had known about it, I would have paid more attention to your threats!" She laughed and said, "Oh Mr. David, you know I wouldn't never hurt you."

> **Step 5:** *Admitted to God, to ourselves, and to another human being the exact nature of our wrongs.*

 # PRINCIPLE: INTEGRITY

You loaded the gun in your inventory through be honest about all of your past. You were afraid to do it, but you gained the principle of courage and you overcame fear. You tapped into the rebellion that you have on the inside and turned it into something positive, rather than using it to say, "I'm not going to follow the rules."

Now you are going to pull the trigger by confessing what you found. There are three different dimensions to the process confessing to God; acknowledging to ourselves, coming clean to another human being, what was really wrong with us and our behaviors. When you have accomplished this triad you will gain a principle called integrity, which will bring you back into a transparent state where people can see who you really are.

The integrity of a building is the measure of its trueness. It means that the infrastructure of the building is sound and firm, and the building is standing erect. It has a plumb line, and it is not going to fall down. If you suffer from an addiction, most likely you have lost your infrastructure. As a result, you no longer have integrity, which is your underpinning and support structure.

How do you recapture your integrity? First you must recognize there are two different people living inside of you as a drug user or alcoholic. One is Reputation Man and the other is Character Man. (Of course, it may be Reputation Woman and Character Woman.) Reputation Man is the person who is out in front. It's the guy who everyone sees. He can become whatever you need for the moment. He is the chameleon, always adapting to the setting so he is not discovered. Reputation Man is the one who will put on a big front. Character man is the person in the background, forever trying to hide from people and reality, hoping that nobody will notice him.

Most alcoholics and addicts fit the description of an egomaniac with an inferiority complex. Can you identify with that? It's Reputation Man and Character Man dueling it out. Part of you is outgoing, with almost overbearing confidence. The other side of you suffers from low self esteem, even lower self worth, and no self image. It's the part of you who would prefer to be alone even when others are around. Alternately, maybe you are a codependent person who relies on those around you for your sense of well being. As a result, you are the counterpart of the egomaniac with the inferiority complex or as I like to put it the control-freak doormat. You are either going to dominate or you are going to let everybody run you into the ground.

The bottom line is that you have two competing personalities. Part of you wants to do the right things, but it can't keep up with the other side, which wants to do the wrong things and make bad choices. You had to split it up so that you could silence your conscience. You learned to turn off your conscious so that you could do whatever was necessary to use alcohol or drugs, or engage in some other addictive behavior. You decided that you were no longer going to listen to any kind of formal standard or rational thinking.

Character Man had to take a backseat, and Reputation Man was out there in front making sure you could get everything that you needed for today by lying, manipulating, and stealing. Reputation Man was slick some days, other days he was angry or just sneaky and trying to get around everything. He was out there doing the job so that you would have something to get high on. People who have been locked up for any period of time know exactly what I am talking about because in prison Reputation Man is important just to stay alive. Reputation is what everybody else sees, but your real character comes into play when you are all alone, and it reflects who you really are. And most people who are addicted don't even know that they have this duality going on inside.

This triad of revealing yourself is the place where Reputation Man finally meets Character Man. It is the point where you suddenly combine these two components of your life and assimilate them back into one person. This reintegration will result in accessing integrity. What you see is what you get. You can't talk about integrity and be a plastic person. You must become transparent so people can see what you have inside and want what you have.

In my years of helping men and women in recovery, I have discovered that when people dig down far enough and become hopeless they become real. And, for the most part, the people who stay in recovery have quality sobriety because they are honest about themselves. If you are phony, other people will start to read through you and shun you, and then you will feel isolation, loneliness, and emptiness, which ultimately will lead you back into your addiction.

This part of the process also is the birthplace of accountability, and that is what is going to hold you fast in sobriety. It might make you nervous, but it is what will make you whole, complete, and transparent. Your willingness to become accountable to God, yourself, and another person is the key to integrating Character Man and Reputation Man. Accountability is bringing your actions, behaviors, and thinking into position so that you can and *must* give an account to someone else.

Accountability provides the following seven things:

1. **Connection with the real you.** No longer can you hide and pretend to be something you are not.

2. **Consistent contact.** Your pattern was self-based addictive

behavior. Self-based recovery just doesn't work. What is needed is "we-based" recovery, which means that you become part of a group—and there is mutual support among its members.

3. **Protection from unrealistic choices and decisions.** In active addiction your choices were built around protecting your sources of alcohol and/or drugs. Allowing someone else into the decision process provides protection from living in a fantasy world.

4. **Solution-based focus.** If you attempt recovery alone you will stay focused in the problems rather than in the solutions. Accountability will provide you access to the resources of others and God and it will help you move forward in sobriety.

5. **Favor and opportunity.** If you draw accountability from people who have achieved long-term sobriety and outlived their own bad reputations, you will have more opportunities. These people tend to have favor in the community and normally have many contacts. It can help open doors that you would not be able to open on your own.

6. **Protection from self-sabotage.** Once you overcome huge obstacles to find employment, a good relationship or a financial posture, you may become fearful and unwittingly destroy what you have put together. Being accountable to others will help you avoid conscious and unconscious self sabotage.

7. **Training for assisting others.** One of the greatest byproducts of finding accountability is that you will learn how to work with and help others.

I already explained earlier that you reap what you sow in life. If you get sober and you stop planting the wrong things, eventually you will stop harvesting a negative crop. In the meantime, instead of complaining about what is wrong, just do what is right. You can't plant corn in the ground and stand there and expect radishes to grow!

While accountability is imperative, it must be coupled with challenge, confrontation, correction, consequences, and closure or it simply is permission to engage in an unacceptable behavior. If you are telling your sponsor that you are doing something questionable and nothing transpires, then the message he or she is sending is that it's OK to continue the behavior. You need to come to a place where you stop getting permission to do the wrong things and face real life.

When someone is there to challenge your actions, it opens communication and brings what is happening out into the open. Confrontation then becomes a tool to motivate actions and results. In turn, this brings about correction, which will move you into the solution and provide alternative behaviors. Consequences then serve as a reminder not to go down the path of negative behavior again. Finally, closure brings an end to a specific episode, allows forgiveness, and helps you to get past the incident.

This is the soul cleansing step. You recognize that deep inside of your soul there is some kind of sickness, something that just never feels quite right. You don't feel comfortable in your own skin when you walk into a room. There is something wrong on the inside and you need to find integrity and make a change.

As a result, this is where you get to meet you. Will the real you please stand up! Many people with addictions have never really met themselves because they are afraid that they will perceive themselves the way they believe other people look at them. Ultimately, what you believe about yourself is determined by what you think other people believe about you. If you think that everybody believes you are a wimp, than inside you believe you are a wimp. That is why you put on the big front and let Reputation Man loose on the world.

I've heard some people say, "It's none of your business what other people think of you." That is a Band-Aid solution to try to help you stop overcompensating and focusing only on what everybody else is saying or thinking. It is not a long-term solution because what you think about what other people think about you is your business, and it is important in many cases. I care what my sons think about me. That's why I am a man of integrity. I care what my boss thinks about me. I care what my sponsor thinks of me, and the list goes on.

I want you to keep in mind that I am not going to stay awake at night worrying what strangers might think about me. But I live my life with integrity because it is imperative that people see me for who I really am. There is a Bible verse that reflects this concept. (Philippians 4:9) "The things you have learned and heard and received and seen in me; Do these things and the God of peace will be with you." This is the pattern we should follow to role model our life of right living so we have nothing to hide.

This is where you get honest with God. If God knows all and is omnipresent, why do you need to admit everything to Him? It's because until you make this effort you have not entered into communication with God. You need to get into the habit of admitting to God the exact nature of your wrongs so that when you go down the road you can pray with confidence that He will hear your prayers. If you don't have that conviction, when you get angry, afraid or frustrated—or you do something that you knew you were not supposed to do—it will put a wedge between you and God and your prayer life will suffer. One day you are praying with great fervor and you have God right there with you, and the next day you are wondering if there even is a God.

However, if you can get to the place where you lay down your life, admit out loud to God what you did, take ownership of it, and ask for forgiveness, then you can stay in the present rather than dwell in the past. As a result, your prayers will begin to launch into the future and establish a spiritual base before you even arrive!

The spoken word has great power, and what you say controls the success or failure of your life. There is a story in the Bible where Jesus is walking with his Disciples and they come upon a fig tree that was supposed to be bearing fruit, but it was empty. Jesus cursed the tree and said that never again would it bear fruit, as they passed by on their journey. This might seem harsh, but there was a lesson Jesus was trying to teach. On the return trip, the tree was withered and dead, and the Disciples remarked about it. Jesus pointed out to them that the words he had spoken had an impact from the spirit realm to the natural realm. It didn't happen instantly, but it manifested over a period of time. When you speak words out of your mouth you create spiritual life and spiritual death, even if the results in the natural world are not instantaneous. You have a choice between life and death. What are you going to speak today?

When you hear yourself admit something out loud you are acknowledging what you did. It is a discipline and a process that will train you to state the truth and understand that you do not need to speak false words ever again. However, you have to draw the line in the sand and say "I'm going to admit the nature of my wrongs to God, to myself, and to somebody else." By doing this your words become potent, powerful, and filled with light, and it will have a dramatic impact when you begin to reveal the second part of your inventory, your positive attributes and traits. This gives way to hopes and dreams, and you will begin to plant your spiritual future, and it will come alive.

It's up to you to decide the best person with whom to share your inventory. But whoever it is, he or she must be a person of integrity, particularly if you did things that were illegal! You need somebody you can trust, somebody who has accountability. I decided to go to a priest because I didn't trust anybody. That was one of my issues. And I went to a priest who was in a recovery program. I was nervous, and he knew it. Then he said, "Most of what you are going to tell me I have already heard, and what I haven't heard I have probably done."

When I would get to something and lower my voice and mumble he would say, "Let's stop and talk about that a little bit." He was pretty slick. When I got done I felt like the world had been lifted off my shoulders, and I came out of there with the confidence that I would never again need to pick up a drink or a drug. I had faith that I could stay sober permanently. Something changed on the inside of me. I had spoken new life into my life with my words. I had left the darkness behind.

Later, however, I began avoiding meetings where I knew the priest attended so I wouldn't have to run into him; some of the things that I said were embarrassing. A few weeks later I went to an entirely new meeting. As I was getting my coffee, I turned around and there he was. He said, "Is this your first time at this meeting? I don't think I've ever met you."

He didn't even remember me! To date I have worked this practice with a lot of people, and I can assure you that most of the time I don't recall any of the details. So don't sweat it. Just make sure you find somebody who you trust so that you can be open and honest.

Here is what I determined in my course of action; I was a full-grown adult who had never taken responsibility for my life or behaviors. I was a self-centered little boy stuck inside of an adult body. At that point I could clearly see that when I escaped from the realities of my life with drugs and alcohol I had stopped growing up. I was still a teenager in my emotions. I didn't know how to live life or have relationships. Any type of success had eluded me. Now, rest assured I didn't figure all of this out in one day, but I was able to glean this insight in time as I continued on in my recovery.

That there is a point in every person's life that there will be nothing that stands between him or her and addiction but a loving God. You need to understand this. When I finally accepted this, I altered my attitude and I changed at the core of my being. I could be myself without fear. You should not be afraid of anything that will put you in touch with the reality of who you are and allow you to become comfortable with yourself. Remember that people judge you by your actions, not your intentions. You might have a heart of gold but so does a hard-boiled egg! Good intentions must be followed by action. In the final analysis we know that, faith without works produces nothing.

"Let integrity and uprightness preserve accountability," says Psalms 25:21. When your character and your reputation, that is who you are and who people perceive you to be, are the same, the secrets that kept you trapped inside are gone. Look not only to lay hold of integrity, but to develop your life with it.

THE TRIAD OF OPENNESS

Confessed to God. Why confess something to God that He already knows? An important piece of the admittance process is discovering that God isn't mad at you. As a result, you build a line of communication with God, and as you come into a relationship with Him you discover you don't have to be afraid anymore.

Admittance is not a one-time thing. The process opens the pathway so that you can talk to God about anything. You can stop living in isolation and in fear. With Step 5 you begin the process of talking to God about everything—right and wrong. It's also a place where you

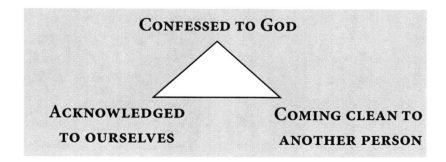

can begin to hear from God and gain spiritual mastery, which is the ability to determine whether you're hearing from God or hearing from yourself. This is not a theoretical God or a historical God. It's not even the God who has sobered up hundreds of thousands of people. It's the God of your experience—it's your personal God.

Acknowledged to ourselves. A large part of self-admission is related to uncovering your motives. It's not about the gory details. It's about looking at your thinking to discover the nature of your wrongs. What is it on the inside of you, what is the dimension of your soul sickness--that has made you the way you are? Why were you so incapable of being honest?

Here, you ask God to empower you so that you can see your true self. It might be unsettling for a period of time, but it will pass if you stay focused. It's also important to tend the seeds you are planting so that they sprout in the future. And don't get discouraged if some weeds crop up along the way. You may have been out there in your addiction for a long time, doing damage and planting bad seeds that have yet to break through the ground. However, if you keep doing good things now, you will reap a healthy harvest down the line.

Coming clean to another person. Notice this doesn't say "to a group of folks." Also, it does little good for you to share part of your story here, there, and anywhere. Pick somebody who knows what he or she is doing and tell the *whole* story. That listener then can communicate with you, confront your behaviors, and challenge you, ultimately making you accountable for your actions.

There was a blonde woman who just couldn't make ends meet financially. She went to church and said, "Lord I am really in desperate shape. All of my credit cards are maxed out, and I'm having challenges in business. I really need help. Lord, would you help me win the Lotto?"

She came back the following Sunday and she said, "Lord, they foreclosed on my business. They are about to take my house away. They may come and repo my car.

I don't have any source of income.

I really need your help. Lord, can I win the Lotto?"

Nothing.

The next week, she goes into church and pleads, "Lord, they have taken my car. I don't have any food for my children. We have to get out of the house by the end of the week. I'm desperate. Please, help me win the Lotto."

At that point a great flash of light came down from the heaven and the Lord said, "Sweetheart work with me. Buy a ticket."

CHAPTER 6

WILLINGNESS

One of the hardest things I had to give up in sobriety was my terrible language. It may seem simple enough, but it was the way I had communicated for a long time, and it was easier said than done.

My first sponsor in recovery was Don Z., and I'm pretty sure he was a Mafia guy; a tough guy for sure, so you can imagine that he was intimidating. He would tell me that I needed to talk in meetings or I was not going to make it. It used to bother me that others were looking at me, and I was embarrassed to talk. I was ashamed. I was always nervous. I was in Ohio at the time, and they used to make you stand up when you spoke at meetings. So one Friday night I got up enough courage to say something. I stood up, and once I got started it was easy. I literally turned the air blue with my offensive language. It was a horrible thing.

When I sat down Don Z. looked me right in the eye and said, "If you ever say another word, I'm going to break both of your legs."

Afterward, he took me out in the alley, and he chewed me out. He said, "I didn't stay sober this long to listen to your filthy mouth. If you can't clean it up, you can't talk in the meetings. And if you don't talk in the meetings, you are not going to stay sober. If you don't stay sober… you figure it out."

I was in the Marines for years. I also drove a truck. I ran around with biker guys when I was drinking. In every crowd I ever associated with I was exposed to that type of unsavory language. I didn't know how to talk without the "F" word. It was an adjective. It was a pronoun;

it was a verb and adjective; I used that word for almost everything in my life, along with a whole array of other words that I need not repeat.

So after enough desperation and self humiliation for saying the wrong things all the time, I asked God to remove profanities from my vocabulary. God answered my prayer and He gave me the ability to talk without offending others and embarrassing myself. Does that mean that I never cursed again, ever? Hell, no! But it does mean that I no longer go into tirades, and I never again will be able to justify or qualify that kind of profanity coming from my mouth.

I used to say, "Pardon my French."

Somebody once replied to me, "It's not French, it's Vulgarity!"

> **Step 6:** *Were entirely ready to have God remove all these defects of character.*

 # PRINCIPLE: **WILLINGNESS**

So now it's time to do something about your problems. It stems directly from your inventory and coming clean about your life; so it is advisable to *step* up to the plate as soon as you finish conducting your inventory and revealing the true nature of your life and problem behaviors. You have identified all the handicaps in your life, looked at all the parts of your world that are not working, and made note of the good things as well. Now it is time to become ready to have God do something about the problems. Why is this necessary? Because if you have successfully worked the steps so far, you understand that you alone are incapable of doing anything about the behavior traits that are destroying your life.

I want you to know that it's not a requirement to hold on to these character defects for the rest of your life, and you are not trapped in a process where you cannot have a complete, full, and successful life. Those who apply the principles within their lives can change permanently so that they no longer have to live in the pathway of destruction. Haven't you had enough pain and misery? And haven't you made enough people who have crossed your path miserable?

In this chapter we are going to look at getting free from a realistic perspective. To do this, I need to talk to you about God so that you can gain a higher understanding of how God works in your life. Do you believe that God loves you? You might not now, but I hope that you will by the time you finish reading this section because if He didn't love you he already would have turned you into toast! He would have come down with a lightning bolt and fried you because you deserved it for all the havoc you created in your life and the lives of those around you. But no doubt He let you survive because you are reading this book, and you are not looking at the grass from the bottom side.

God cares about you, and He wants you to know that he cares about you. He has a plan for your life. Did you know that? He has a purpose and a destiny for your life. You weren't born by mistake in this life to do nothing. God did not intend for you to end up as an alcoholic or addict and screw up your life. Rest assured that God has something better for you. If he didn't then He would not have given you a pathway or process so that you could get out of this mess. He didn't rescue you from drowning in the ocean to beat you up on the beach.

I know some people believe that everything is exactly the way it is supposed to be all the time, everybody is right where they are supposed to be all the time, and all things are perfect, amen. I'll bet you have heard this at some point in recovery. However, if this is true then everything is predestined and there is no free will. I don't believe that anybody deserves to become an alcoholic or a drug addict, and it wasn't predestined. It wasn't God's idea. It wasn't God's plan. It was your plan.

Here is the deal: God did come up with a plan and a purpose for your life—and it preceded your addiction. And He still has that plan and it will come back into focus when you break the cycle of addiction. God did not change His plan because you were out messing around, and that plan was for you to succeed in life.

God's will for you must come into play at this point in the process. It will resurface again over and over, but I need to introduce it here so that you understand that there is God's will and then there is your will; your will is what got you into this mess in the first place. Your freewill is part of who you are, what you believe, how you think, and what you decide to do. Your free will also is the culprit when it comes to addiction. Say to yourself: "It wasn't God's will, it was my will. It wasn't God's plan, it was my plan. It wasn't God's purpose, it was my purpose. That is how I became addicted."

The paradox also is true: Your freewill can get you out of your addiction. God will empower your freewill to make the right choices and the right decisions, and He will free you from everything that you want to remove from your life. Consider this: If everything is just the way it's supposed to be all the time, then where is the reward for good character, integrity, and honor? What is the reward for perseverance, diligence, and hard work? If everything is exactly the way it is supposed to be all the time, then go out tonight to the bar and get drunk and say it was God's idea.

The bottom line is that this is an exercise in freewill. You have become entirely ready, stepped into that purpose, and stepped into that plan. This place and principle of willingness now must be addressed. The first part of willingness is your will. What you believe makes you who you are. You are not designed or defined by what you feel. You are defined by what you believe, and that is at the core of your freewill.

Imagination is at the root of emotions and the soul, and the part of you that is most like God is your imagination. God is a creator, and He gave you the innate ability to create. You have one little thought and then you create all types of scenarios with your freewill, and there are two irrefutable facts that you need to know about this process. The first is that God gave you a freewill that He will never override. He will not come down and snatch the pills out of your hand. The second is that the moment that you ask God to empower your freewill to make the right choices and the right decisions, He empowers you. Isn't that good news?

When you take your will to the next level you become willing, and willing is the active tense of will. As a result, willing is an application of your choice. Moreover, when you make the right choice and finally realize that God's design and plan is better than your design and plan, you move from a place of willing to a posture of willingness—a perpetual state of existence produced by your choice. In summary, will is your choice, willing is the application of your choice, and willingness is the state being produced by your choices. Willingness is the activation of will, where you put something into motion, and you go to any length.

As a result of completing this surrender, I have the willingness to personally do whatever it takes to help myself and other people stay sober permanently. That willingness came once I discovered that God's will was greater than my will, and I realized that I was a decent individual with dreams and hopes that I could achieve if I just stepped up to the plate. If it were not for your freewill, you would not be able to identify God's will. If it were not for your unwillingness, you would not be able to identify willingness. To clarify this point, let me ask you these questions:

- What are you willing to do to change your life?

- Are you willing to go to meetings?

- Are you willing to get help?

- Are you willing to get a mentor or sponsor who wants to help you reclaim you life?

- Are you willing to pray?

- Are you open and willing to change how you handle money, work, and relationships?

Now let's look at the opposite side of the equation. **What is the one thing that you are not willing to change?** This is the key to transforming your life. The one thing that you will not or cannot change on your own is what will keep you locked in the prison of addiction. I can't say it enough times: The one thing that you are not willing to do is going to be your stumbling block in this process. When you get to this juncture you must be totally prepared to have God take away *all* of your character flaws, that means every one; it's all inclusive. The one that you are not ready to have God remove will haunt you, so you need to get rid of it while the getting is good! There seems to be some type of supernatural grace that is extended the first time you go through the process, and the more thoroughly you do this the better your results will be in the long term.

Maybe the one thing you are not willing to give up is profane language? "I am going to curse like a drunken sailor because I can if I want to..." Maybe you decided to hold on to lust because you believe that if you give it up you will lose your sex desire. Analyze why you want to hold on to this thing. What does it produce for you? Why does it make you feel good? Do you feel good after looking at pornography on the Internet for five hours? Get honest with yourself and admit whether a behavior makes you feel remorse, guilt, and shame. Why? Because that is how addiction makes you feel.

Again this is about having God remove all failings that have plagued you for so long. We are not talking about modifying behaviors. We are not talking about God giving you strength for a daily acquittal so that you don't have to go back into a particular state of existence. It's not a modification, it's a removal. It's not put it on the shelf and pick it up later. It is to disassociate with, to cut it away, to take it off.

Everything that I have ever been willing to let go of God was willing to remove. He removed every personality imperfection that I had when I started in recovery. If you hear people tell you they are stuck with the state they are in and have the same problems they had when they stopped drinking or using drugs, tell them to access willingness! To help you avoid this pitfall yourself, here are the top 10 things that will keep you from being entirely willing to have God remove *all* of the temperament imperfections from your life.

The fear of change. Do you know why you don't like change? It's because you don't know what something is going to look like once it's changed. And you're probably assuming that when it changes it is going to change for the worse, to your disadvantage, because you believe that you are a victim of circumstance. You are a subscriber to the idea that life is not fair, and you are correct. Life is not always fair, but God is always just.

I didn't quit smoking for a long time after I became sober because I didn't know what it would be like to go to a recovery meeting or hang around with my friends without cigarettes. I didn't want to let go of smoking because I thought there was some great connection to society in it. However, I knew it was awful for my body, so I said to God, "Take away the desire, and I will throw away the cigarettes." And I prayed every day, and I stopped feeling guilty about it. I used to leave my cigarettes in the kitchen and pray in the living room thinking maybe God wouldn't notice!

The desire left just after I bought a whole carton of cigarettes. I said, "NOW?" At first I thought I would smoke those and then quit, and then I decided that God had already removed the desire and that would be going back on my word. He cut His part of the deal. Did it go from zero to 100 percent of me that didn't want to smoke? Not really. I went to about 85 percent to 90 percent of me that didn't want to smoke anymore, and I had to tell that 10-plus percent of me that did want to light up to shut up. That was January 1985. I firmly believe if I had played with a modification and finished those cigarettes it would not have worked.

Not forgiving. Who have you not forgiven? Let go of it all. Forgive it all. Don't wait until you think the other person has changed and is ready to forgive you because he or she may never change and may never be ready. Forgiveness is not conditional upon somebody's ability or desire to change. Forgiveness is an inside job. And by the way, forgiveness is not an event, it is a process. How many times are you supposed to forgive, perhaps seven times in a day? No! The answer is as many times as necessary. It could be seven times 70, which is 490 times a day. If you want to break it down, that's about every two minutes.

A feeling of inadequacy. There are three basic emotional needs that everyone has: a sense of belonging, a sense of competence, and a sense of worthiness. The feeling of inadequacy encompasses all three of these elements in a personal void. This inadequacy, not feeling worthy, not being good at anything and not fitting in, produces self pity and a victim mentality. The internal impression you get is that you are not at fault and there is nothing you can do about it.

The quick-fix mentality. This is desiring something that will make you feel good right now to take away all pain and discomfort. This, of course, is an extremely short fix, especially when it comes to alcohol and drugs, and their use is followed by even greater discomfort and pain. This also encompasses all addictive behaviors, from bad relationships to gambling to food. These quick fixes hold some form of relief and that is why people still use them!

A lack of knowledge. You need to pray to receive insight, and it is about asking. "You have not because you ask not. And you receive not because you ask in error, wishing to consume it upon your own desires." (James 4:3) You can have anything you want, anything you request from God, if your motives are right and you are prepared to receive. I have heard it said, "Watch what you pray for because you just might get it. This indicates that you might get more than you bargained for. However, I maintain that God never gives you more than you can handle; either good or bad. Perhaps those who purport the "watch what you pray for" idea should consider that what you don't pray for you will never get. Pray for willingness, or if you are not there yet pray for the willingness to become willing.

Lack of faith to believe that it will last. When you remove fear, for example, you are afraid it will come back. Fear is not an internal emotional, it is an external driver. God has not given you a spirit of fear, but an essence of love, power, and a sound mind. That is what God wants you to have. When God removes something He replaces it with something better. So let go of the fear.

Other people's influence. This includes all of the people who say they have been sober forever and still have all of their old behaviors. When they try to influence you to believe that you are stuck with your defects forever say, "I am not stuck with them!"

Procrastination. You put things off. "I'll do it later," or "I'll do it this weekend." Procrastination is a big trap. Enough said. Just do it!

Denial. Don't go back into denial. You've been in six jails in four states. You can't keep a job for more than a month, and you've been drinking a fifth of vodka a day for as long as you can remember. You have cirrhosis of the liver and Hepatitis C. Nobody will talk to you. And you don't believe you have an alcohol or drug problem? Denial. Need I say more?

Pride. If you fall back into your addiction, you can bet that pride preceded the relapse and caused the ensuing path of destruction. You had a big attitude. You developed an arrogant spirit. If nothing else, you got prideful enough to think that God was not big enough to resolve your problems. Pride will take you out of your relationship with God. Pride will tell you that you know better than everybody else.

God is an essential part of this progression. What He can do and what He will do, are the same thing. You may say to yourself, well I know God can do anything, but I doubt he will. If you believe this you are wrong. He will if you will straighten up. He will if you will connect your will to His will. You can have a reasonable expectation that God is qualified to participate in your change. God can remove whatever character flaws you are completely prepared to give up and still leave you whole on the inside and outside. God will participate in this process with you. He has a plan, and He is qualified to participate in your life; remember He is omnipresent (everywhere at once), omnipotent (all powerful), and omniscient (all knowing). He is more than qualified, more than enough to meet your needs.

A drunk was sitting at the bar, and a lady walked into the bar
with a poodle on her arm. She came up and sat down
next to him. The drunk looked over, squinted at her,
and asked, "Hey, where'd you get the pig?"
The lady got indignant and said, "I'll have you know, sir,
that this is not a pig. This is a poodle."
He answers, "Well, I'll have you know that
I was talking to the poodle."

CHAPTER 7
HUMILITY

Of all of the things that will produce humility in your heart, perhaps there is nothing greater than wanting to help one of your own children, one you would give up your own life for–and then finding out you are powerless to do anything to change the circumstances. I have met parents who went through the battle of long-term illness with a child; observed vicious custody battles where the child loses the most and attorneys are the only people better for the process; stood with parents graveside mourning the loss of a child; and worked with parents who have dearly loved children in the throes of addiction. I have seen the humility that is birthed out of such suffering through my work with others, and I also have my own tale, one that personally ingrained a new understanding of humility for me.

The walk of life with my oldest son and namesake has been precarious at best. David proved to have above average intelligence as a child. He was outgoing, creative, and a natural leader and salesman. He was usually a step ahead of me in most pursuits. The two things that took David down the wrong path were my tragic and aggressive divorce coupled with years of custody battles, and then his own early encounters with drug and alcohol abuse.

David was in and out of the juvenile legal system, and an array of schools and programs did not reach him. The prayers of many didn't turn him around, although I am not saying I have given up hope. (It's not over till it's over, and I am still praying.) If you stay in the devil's orchard long enough there you will reap the fruit, and eventually trouble occurred. David was 15 at the time. The charges were serious enough to merit prison time, and research showed that in many similar cases three to five years was the average sentence. We battled in court for three years, and David was in a county jail the entire time.

They finally offered us 10 years on a plea bargain. Ten years seemed too long for a kid of 18! He had multiple charges, but nobody died or sustained serious injury. Was he wrong? Of course. Did he deserve to pay for what he did? Sure. But it seemed too harsh, and in the end we turned it down.

The day finally came when I stood with my 18 year old son for the sentencing. We stated our case and the victim did the same. I could not believe what I heard as the judge began a pompous tirade. On the first charge the court sentenced him to 50 years. I nearly passed out. Perhaps the judge had a grievance to air, maybe he had political advantage to gain, maybe he was paid off? It all ran through my head. I stood helpless as my son David was sentenced to a cumulative total of 90 years. I stood and watched hopelessly as they took him away. So vivid and painful was this moment that I weep now writing about it.

The questions later turned to anger, and I had to pray earnestly for the judge and the legal team that, in such a cavalier manner, sent this teenager to prison for a lifetime of unjustifiable punishment. I refused to become the victim and prayed until the anger melted away. I have concluded that God is always sovereign, but people are often wrong and sometimes unintelligent and more times than not self-serving.

Humiliation comes through my own actions, humility comes through life circumstances. I was humbled through this episode.

Step 7: *Humbly asked Him to remove our shortcomings.*

PRINCIPLE: HUMILITY

This is not talking about your neighbor, your boss, or your sponsor. It's not talking about any human being. When we speak of God it is common to use the term "Him". But don't get hung up on the pronoun and develop a resentment because it is expressing the male gender. It's written that way in the Bible, and I'm not about to rewrite anything here. However, God is not gender based. God is a spirit, and as a part of this spiritual dynamic I will continue to use Him. I say this as we start discussing this part of the process, because I don't want you to get hung up on a male vs. female debate and lose sight of what you are trying to accomplish.

When we ask Him, that is God and I need to humble my heart to expect an answer. I don't apologize to anyone for talking about God, and I'm not afraid of God today, or anyone's opinion of me for my beliefs. God is my friend and constant companion. He cares about me, loves me, and has demonstrated Himself to me over and over again. And God talks to me all of the time. You might say that sounds a little bit nutty, but it's not any crazier than you talking to yourself all the time, which you know you do!

Let's go back to our discussion on willingness for a minute. To remove is to extract, take away, eradicate, or eliminate. That does not mean modify, adjust, or gain control over. It's not to get a daily reprieve from your bad behaviors. Why do you want to hold on to them anyway? They are the things that destroyed your life and caused the downward spiral that landed you in recovery. It's time to let go of the things that are keeping you from having a life second to none. You don't have to drink anymore. You don't have to use drugs anymore. You don't have to go out and get high and destroy your life, go to jail, or crash your car. You don't have to spend money that you don't have. You don't have to steal money so you can spend money that you don't have. You can learn how to stay sober. To do this, you must humbly approach God, rather than address Him with arrogance. The principle of

85

course is humility, and it is central to your recovery; if you don't have it the rest will disappear. People who relapse became filled with pride first. They thought they knew everything, they knew they were above the principles, and they believed the rules didn't apply to them.

Most addicts are struggling in life, trying to figure out how to survive. They have plans and think they know the right direction, but then somehow they get off the pathway and there is pain, suffering, turmoil, and agony. As a result, they decide they need something to help get them through, usually alcohol or drugs. This mode not only allows but mandates that they put on some sort of false front or façade, which we talked about in chapter 5; recall our friend, Reputation Man. They also recognize themselves as a victim and they posture themselves that way so that people take advantage of them and abuse them. A lot of the behaviors associated with this cycle are self imposed later in life.

Maybe this describes you. If it does, you probably feel that one day you are going to get up and it's going to be different. One day you are not going to be in so much pain or turmoil. Something is going to change, and you are going to feel like you belong somewhere. But in this process you keep building walls and pride keeps getting in the way, especially if somebody is trying to help you. Pride says don't let your guard down because that person is going to abuse you too. And that pride becomes a festering nemesis. There is nothing in your life more insidious, natural, destructive, permanent, invisible or real than pride, and it can destroy you. It will eat you up from the inside out.

Some of the most prideful people that I have ever met are homeless and live in the woods. Each night they reexamine themselves, realign themselves, and pull up the walls of pride. I've seen people live on mattresses in squalor by railroad tracks. I've been to 40 homeless camps in Sarasota County, Florida, many more than one time. I know most of the homeless people in my area by name. I've told many of them that I've got a bed for you, and we can help at our facility. The response typically is, "Oh, well, I don't think I'm that bad yet." How can you not call that pride?

The useless destructive aspects of your personality that cause pain and misery are mired in a seedbed of arrogance. And you work hard to hold on to those useless flaws, those shortcomings and faults. You don't know how to let go, and you don't know what to let go of. However, it's not hopeless when you attain humility.

Humility is nothing but the disappearance of self and the realization that God is all. God is either everything or He is nothing. In other words, either there is a God or there isn't a God. I was told early on, "There is a God and it's not you!" Today, I believe that. Humility is about giving up self reliance. At the core of the dilemma, at the core of this thing called addiction, is selfishness, self centeredness, self will, and this self life is destructive. You were trying to function the only way you knew how to function, but it was all based around a foundation of fear.

In an interesting paradox, however, self centeredness cannot be broken without first identifying it as self centeredness. There is a great saying that I heard and purposed to remember. It goes like this, that selfishness is never so exquisitely selfish as when it's on its knees. You are more selfish than you ever thought you could be when you begin to pray. As you come into recovery, you come out of the world of addiction and chaos and you begin to consider prayer. You may go down on your knees, but at this point you have not moved very far. You are just selfish on a different level. Using your mind and emotions, you have taken selfishness and placed it over into the spiritual realm. You begin to ask God for the impossible: Help me win the Lottery! This will change in time.

There is a verse in the Bible that says, "Humble yourself in the sight of the lord and He will lift you up." (James 4:10) This is an act of your free will and refers to a posture that you can choose to enter into. If humility is a choice, then it is a characteristic or a virtue that can be possessed and understood. Here's the real deal: If you think you have humility, and if you learn what humility is, and if you embrace it as part of your lifestyle, then you have humility. In other words, don't pay any attention to the old slogan, "If you think you have humility, you have lost it."

Let me tell you a story about humility. I grew up in a small town, and I went to a Pentecostal church where the music was just awful.

The piano was out of tune and some of the keys just made a "plink" sound. For a young boy who liked music, it made listening to the songs a very painful experience. And when the pastor would announce that there was going to be some special music, that (we'll call them) Brother Stanley and Sister Ethel were going to come up and sing, I knew it was going to be really horrible because they couldn't carry a tune. They would always use self-deprecating comments such as, "Now remember to listen to the words, not how we sing." They believed they were humble because they put themselves down. But they were wrong because pride had them groveling trying to be humble. Pride or maybe ignorance had them up in front of a room doing something they had no talent to do.

I would like to clarify something for you. There is a difference between humility and stupidity. Self denunciation and self abhorrence are not humility. Negative things that you say about yourself still are still after all, all about you! Self denunciation is still about self and in the long run you can't defeat self-centeredness with self-centeredness. You cannot find humility by walking in pride. The correct thing to do is to acknowledge that every talent, gift, and good thing in you came from God.

Rather than denounce yourself for what you cannot do, you have to identify your talents and then thank God for them. Twenty-five years ago speaking was not my forte. It was a skill that I had to develop. Now I'm no longer afraid to speak. I feel certain that I have a God given talent to speak and humor to go with it. Well at least I don't put people to sleep - - - much. I'm not bragging about this ability. God gave it to me, and I recognize that. God is always with me when I get up to talk. Humility is acknowledging that every capability I have came from God.

You need to acknowledge what God has done for you and through you. Furthermore, you can say that you have humbled yourself before God, and you know that is the right thing to do. However, just telling someone that you have humbled yourself before God is not a sufficient demonstration that you have actually done it. As a matter of fact, I would take it one step further and say that the only proof and evidence that you have humbled yourself before God is demonstrated in your ability to humble yourself before men.

"How can you say you love God who you have not seen,
when you hate your brother, who you have seen"? (I John 4:20)

Pride and humility are the two master powers that fight for the possession of your thoughts, words, and actions. When you repent from sins, the errors and faults that you have--you come into right standing with God. However, this will not hold you firm in the long run if you have not repented from pride into humility. This is because pride says I will get by with whatever I want to do. Pride says I'm not hurting anybody but myself. It says I will never get caught, I know better, I am smarter, I am quicker, and I am slicker. Pride will tell you that you are going to get away with whatever it is you want to do.

Let me share with you a quote from one of my favorite books on the subject: "Humility is the only soil in which the graces root. The lack of humility is the sufficient explanation of every defect and failure." The book is called "Humility" and it was written by Andrew Murray in 1871. If you walk in humility all the graces are available to you including faith, gentleness, meekness, kindness, temperance, goodness, and charity. They all grow in the soil of humility.

You can have a lot of knowledge but not have enough wisdom to walk with humility. Knowledge is just information. Wisdom is the application of that information in your life. In my own experience, I have found that there are eight things that will produce humility:

Personal failure. Some of the failures in my life truly have helped me. As just one example, I want to go back to my recovery program on the East Coast of Florida, which I talked about in Chapter 3. We had great people. The place was always full, and the church was packed on Sunday. I owned a large apartment building that paid the bills, and I was living in a 4,200-square-foot house on an acre and a half of land. I thought I had it all. But pride and self centeredness got in the way and infighting among the board ultimately destroyed the dream. I lost everything: the rehab center, the apartment building, and my house.

As a result, my next job was driving a fish bait delivery truck. You can trust me when I tell you this was an ego-reducing position. The truck was raggedy, the pay was poor, and everywhere I went people said, "Here comes that smelly guy." So I learned how to be kind to people even when they were nasty to me. The humiliation of being put down and looked down upon can make you bitter or make you better. If you embrace humility and don't waste the pain you will get better.

There is a huge difference between humility and humiliation. Humility comes from an internal source and humiliation comes from the outside. Have you ever been humiliated? If so, you probably were embarrassed and you wanted to crawl under the table. They both come from the same root word. One (humiliation) comes from doing the wrong thing in front of people the other one (humility) comes from doing the right thing in front of God.

Being in the company of great men. Great men walk in humility and possess the character to ignore notoriety and fame so they can be of service to others. One great man who influenced me is trumpet player Phil Driscoll. In many opinions, he is one of the greatest trumpet players on the planet, and a couple of years ago he even opened for the Grammy Awards. He walked out on the stage with his trumpet and he got a standing ovation from the crowd. One year he came and helped us with an outreach in Florida at the Daytona Bike Week. This was a man who could go anywhere he wanted to go and perform wherever he desired. However, he chose to fly into Daytona on his own airplane to help connect to bikers who were looking for change in their lives.

Another great man in my life was one of my sponsors, Walt Wiries, who died at 53 years sober. Walt knew more about recovery than anyone I have ever met. He had what was fondly known as the "Drunks, Pirates, and Jailbirds Ministry." He was the chaplain for the Pittsburg Pirates baseball team and had a jail ministry, but you would never know it. I would visit his home and he would make a little popcorn and chat like he had nothing much to say. However, his wisdom was always just below the surface. He seemed to have the right thing to say at the right time. He taught me about the recovery principles and how to teach them to others, and I owe him thanks for his influence in this book.

People you have tried to help who fail. Watching others relapse is the No. 1 reason people give up on the service aspect of recovery. I have seen people fail and destroy all that they have put together. I have watched people go to prison, and I have buried others. Rather than throwing in the towel, each time you see addiction take a person back out you should be humbled to know that you have somehow been graced by God to remain free of that lifestyle.

Human fallibility in the shadow of God's providence. If you are aware that God's greatness is beyond all human comprehension, you will feel small in His eyes. Knowing that an all powerful, eternal God has the desire to have a relationship with me, a person among billions of people currently on the earth (to say nothing of all who have been here before and are yet to come) is humbling. The fact that God knows all about me and hears my prayers makes me feel awe.

Gifts given into your life. Having gratitude for all that is good in your life will help you remain humble. I can't even write down all of the gifts God has given to me, but my children definitely are at the top of the list. I have a wonderful job, good health, and many friends. Plus, fear has been removed from my life as a result of working my recovery program.

Tragedy. Nothing is more powerful in producing a humble heart than walking through personal tragedy. When all of your money disappears, divorce comes, and the loss of someone you love hits you, humility will follow with the right attitude. As I stated before, it will make you bitter or it will make you better. Never waste your pain. Allow it to shape your character.

Gracefully receiving honor. In the past I have been honored to be a keynote speaker, given awards in the military, and celebrated for academic achievements. I know I didn't do it alone. How you respond to situations such as this will produce either wrongful pride or humility.

Taking pride in your achievements is different than being prideful. The prideful person takes all of the credit for the position of honor, while the humble individual shares the acclaim with others who showed support and encouragement.

God's answers and time. Direct contact with The Creator of the Universe should produce humility in your heart. However, the amount will depend on how much you actually believe in God. If God is nothing more than a theory in your mind, then you will not spend much time in His presence and the answers to your questions will be elusive. If you actually believe that God rewards those who pursue Him, then the prospect of direct contact should be exciting. Knowing and believing that God hears me and answers me in ways that no human possibly can is a humbling experience.

I want to close the discussion on humility with this story. I grew up in New York, and it snowed nonstop throughout the winter. Sometimes the drifts would get so high I couldn't even see my house when I drove down the road in front of it. When the snow was coming, I would listen to a little transistor radio and tune in one of the AM stations waiting to hear the words "snow day." When I heard them, I knew I got to stay home from school. And there was something special about snow days. It wasn't like having another day off. It was unique because I got a reprieve. On that day everything changed in an instant. I didn't have to contend with all of the pressures of school. I could do anything I wanted to do for the rest of the day. For the next several hours I could watch whatever I wanted to watch on TV. I could go out and get cold in the snow, and then come in and get hot, and then go back out and get cold again. I didn't have to think about all the stuff that frightened me.

The same is true for you today if you are ready to embrace humility. You don't have to wonder how you are going to get by using drugs or alcohol and not get arrested. You don't need to worry where you are going to get money for drugs, alcohol, gambling, pornography, or any other addiction. You know you are going to have enough food. It is a reprieve from all the pressures of addiction and that lifestyle. You have a reprieve today. It is a snow day. All you have to do is humbly ask Him to remove your shortcomings.

The Proof and Rewards of Attaining Humility

Removal of groveling. You no longer need to apologize for the gifts that God has bestowed upon you.

Broken spirit. Unlike broken emotions, this is the internal ability to be moved by external stimulus, both positive and negative. A person who has a broken spirit has the ability to be moved by things that the average person wouldn't. It goes beyond the emotion to a higher spiritual understanding.

Dependence on God. You know that everything in your life is reliant on God's love, grace, and power.

"Teachability." A person who is filled with pride lacks the capacity to be taught. Humble people are eager to learn. You have both the faculty and the desire to expand your knowledge base.

Compassion. Urgency, understanding, and sympathy are the markings of a compassionate person. You are always moving toward the greatest need, motivated by your own experience.

Favor. You are given opportunities in life that wouldn't exist without the influence of another. When you have favor for a moment you are the favorite.

Contentment. This is not the absence of goals or desires, but the appreciation for all that you have and all that you are. You can enjoy the moment right where you are.

No need to compete. You are not caught up in the need to outdo someone else.

Ability to hear others. If you are humble, you have good listening skills.

Meekness. You are bashful on purpose and understand that appropriate recognition will come in the right time.

Happiness. You are happy with life and enjoy what you are doing. You don't require others to entertain you.

Respect. It is evident you respect others' beliefs, stations in life, and desires. When you give respect you receive it back.

Self control. This is the absence of self-initiated chaos. You choose and move deliberately.

Peace. This is the absence of conflict and turmoil in your life. It is not the disappearance of all disorder, but you have tranquility in the midst of life's challenges and trials.

Appreciation. This is a genuine like for variety in everything from food to music to culture. You are open to seeing the good in all things.

Likeableness. You are a friendly outgoing person.

Promotion in life. You are promoted in life because you do a good job and practice diligence in all aspects of your life.

Lack of anger. Similar to peace, you are not moved to anger or frustration by unimportant matters.

There was a big shot New England attorney who decided he was going to go turkey hunting in Texas. He was all decked out with his gun, and he saw a turkey sitting up in a tree. He pulled up and shot the turkey, and it fell on the other side of a fence. So he took out his wire cutters to cut the fence and get the turkey.

When he was just about to make the first cut a famer showed up and said, "What are you doing?"

He said, "I shot that turkey, that's my turkey, and I'm coming over to get it."

"First of all, you can't cut my fence and, second, it's not your turkey," the farmer replied.

The attorney got angry: "Yes it is! I shot it."

"That doesn't matter. It's on my property, so it's my turkey."

"Well apparently you don't know who you are dealing with. I am one of the most powerful litigation attorneys in all of New England, so you had better give me my turkey."

"Apparently you don't understand how things are done around here because that turkey is on my property and now it's my property."

"I beg to differ." The attorney was getting really mad now.

"You can beg to differ if you want. You just don't understand how we do things.

"Well how do you do things?" the lawyer asked.

"Here we use the three kick method to determine property rights."

"What in the world is that?"

The farmer looked at him in the eye and said, "It's like this. I kick you three times, and then you kick me three times, and I kick you three times, and you kick me three times. We go back and forth until one of us gives and the other one gets the turkey."

The lawyer thought about it for a minute and thought, "You are an old man I can beat you anytime."

So the attorney went over the fence and the old man came up and kicked him right in the side of the leg. He fell over and grabbed his leg and the old man kicked him in his side. Then he kicked him in the back of the head. The attorney was lying on the ground writhing in pain. The old farmer went and sat down on a stump.

The attorney got up, and he was really mad. "All right it's my turn!"

Then the farmer said, "Aw, I give. You can have the turkey."

96

CHAPTER 8

BROTHERLY LOVE

In the early 90s I became heavily involved in working with street-level homeless people. I was serving as the Founding Chairman of the County's Homeless Coalition and The Mayor's Feed the Hungry Program, as well as serving on other boards and as a pastor. I felt a calling toward the homeless, and I had a desire to help alleviate their plight. If you had asked me at the time whether I had compassion, I would have said absolutely.

Each morning I taught a class on turning your life around to 25-30 hardcore homeless men and women. Most of them were unkempt, some were still drunk from the night before, and all were desperate. My primary focuses were to teach them how to give in their lives and not just always be on the take and to understand the principle of reaping what you sow. To demonstrate this, each morning I would pass the basket and people would drop in a few coins, a book of matches, and an even an occasional dollar bill.

This went on for about three months, and one day a homeless man in the class asked what I was doing with the money. I told the whole group I had been saving it up, and it was now time for them to decide how to spend it. It was approaching Christmastime, and my thoughts were to buy something that could be distributed among all of the homeless. However, I gave them the authority to choose what they would spend the pool of $140 on. They came back to me with a surprise that moved my heart.

Someone spoke up for the group and said, "There is a homeless family living in their car, and we want to spend the money on gifts for the three children."

They had learned the lesson I was trying to teach, and it was very rewarding for me. I sent a homeless man and a volunteer to go buy gifts. You know you wouldn't send two homeless with the money. All of the homeless who had been donating to the pool of money came for the wrapping session. The day came when all of the homeless folks gathered, and the homeless family was brought in to their great Christmas surprise. Mom, Dad and the kids. It was so moving it brought tears to my eyes. Here they were, homeless people helping a homeless family. On that day my ideas and understanding of compassion expanded and deepened. It has had an impact that carries through to all of my work today. It was the greatest demonstration of brotherly love I have ever seen.

> **Step 8:** *Made a list of all persons we had harmed, and became willing to make amends to them all.*

PRINCIPLE: BROTHERLY LOVE

Here is the juncture where you permanently break the back of self centeredness, which has been at the core of your addiction. It was about you being selfish every moment of every day in everything that you did. It was always all about you. This is a call for you to begin to show a little love and make a list of those people to whom you are ready and willing to make reparation with. It should not be confused with the list of the people to whom you eventually will be making atonement with. This love is demonstrated in a comprehensive list of all people you have harmed and the affirmation that you are willing to make things right with them. In doing so, you must embrace the principle of brotherly love.

Now you are ready to round the bend and say that you are going to apply what you have learned in the first seven principles so that you can get outside of self and get centered on other people. No doubt, you will stay sober on fear in early recovery because everybody that comes out of addiction is plagued with lots of different types of fear. You are in bewilderment. You are confused. Some of you are staying sober now because you are afraid of your dope dealer; you owe him more money than you can count. You are afraid that you are going to go out there in the world, relapse, and die. Some of you have spent two or three decades in prison, and you are afraid that you are going to end up back there. Some of you have destroyed almost everything in your lives, and you are hanging on to your family by a thread, and you are afraid that you are going to lose them. These are examples of fear-based recovery.

At some point you have to say, "I have stayed sober through fear long enough." Now it is time to let go of that fear and to begin to replace it with faith. It will require that you stop focusing on you, and start focusing on others. This is a turning point on this journey through the recovery process. What I am talking about in taking this action is moving from fear to love. It is when you stop running from things and start running toward something.

In my recovery, this rehabilitation process that I have focused on for 30 years, it has been about looking outside of myself and not just zeroing in on me. Remember the idea is to get well, whole, and complete, and then begin to help other people. By doing this a cycle of life free from addiction is established.

It's hard to delve into talking about this principle of brotherly love, without some discussion on trust. Without trust there is no love. Trust precedes love, and true love in any kind of relationship requires trust. This is part of the reason you have been unable to form healthy relationships; you don't know how to trust. Trust involves risk. You need to learn how to take risks and break up all those unhealthy patterns that have developed during years of addiction.

To take healthy risks and trust, you must be trustworthy yourself. You get trust in your life when you become worthy of it. Are you still lying? Gossiping? Stealing? Are you trustworthy in the promises you make? You know on the inside whether you are trustworthy. There is a psychic change, and divine intervention is expressed into and through you until you have a posture of trust and worth. What you see in early sobriety is a person who might hear 10 compliments and one criticism in a single day. He or she then holds onto the *one* negative thing. If this describes you, then you are not in a posture of trust and worthiness because you don't evaluate people based on who they are—you evaluate people based on who *you* are. That's why people who are in recovery identify so strongly with other people in recovery. Mostly used in a negative connotation is the old adage, If you spot it, you got it. But the same holds true in a positive way. The more trust you have in recovery and the other people in recovery, the more trust you will express in the world.

Today, I have love for alcoholics and addicts. However, when I tell a group in recovery I love them it is a different type of love than I express for my sons or you might show for a spouse or parent. It's also different from the kind of love I experience when I'm in prayer with God. This type of love found in recovery circles is known as *philia* in Greek, and it means brotherly love. The name Philadelphia is derived from this word, and it is known as "The City of Brotherly Love". This love, as are all types of love, is based on some dimension of trust, and this trust is developed over time.

The feeling of safety in a relationship comes with trust that is based on the power of your own vulnerability—your own transparency will cause others to feel safe around you. Know this, that you can't compartmentalize trust. This is why relationships are discouraged in early sobriety. You're not capable of trust; therefore you're not capable of a relationship. When you sober up, you start feeling good again. You might start thinking about romance, but before you dive in you need to go through the process and get these principles working in your life. Early on you're still too damaged from your previous relationships to know how to trust yourself or trust others, let alone stay sober. If a relationship is framed within dishonesty, it is doomed to failure.

In this process, you also must understand that finding love and trust is not about jumping forward, figuring out the people you want to talk to and the ones you don't want to address. I'd like you to forget for a minute that there even is a need to ever approach anyone to right the wrong.

This process is *only* about making a list of people that you have harmed. Who have you harmed? Physically who have you harmed? If you are a man maybe you were aggressive and you knocked people around, such as people you were in relationships with. Unfortunately, my personal experience has shown that many addicts have been physically abusive toward their children as a result of the crazy, self-centered lives they have lived. And some may not have hurt children physically, but they had a negative impact on them mentally and emotionally. Or you might have hurt your mom or your dad. You broke promises to them over and over again.

The harm you have done will fall into four categories: physical, mental, emotional, or spiritual. In the case of the latter, for example, if you knew better and you didn't train your children in some type of spiritual life then you neglected to do something that you should have done. That is wrong, and it caused spiritual harm. It is not just about what you did, the sins of commission, but it also is about the sins of omission, the things that you didn't do that you knew you should have done. Every person in addiction skipped things that he or she should have done in their lives that caused other people harm on different levels.

Again, it brings you to the day of internal reckoning where you need to make a list of everybody who you harmed. Some people don't know if they can do this. Understand that every excuse you can make at this point is pride based. As I explained in Chapter 7, pride goes before destruction, and a haughty spirit precedes a fall. You need the principle of humility, and you must put it into motion. You can't reach out and help other people until you humble yourself, and the only evidence that you have humbled yourself in the sight of the Lord is when you have humbled yourself in the sight of men.

There is nothing more humbling than walking into the process of looking headlong at all the people that you have harmed. And trust me, everybody who has suffered from an addiction has harmed somebody at some point. When I started making my list it was short. It was what came immediately to mind and it was short because I was lazy. However, I needed to begin to walk back through my life and look at everybody I actually harmed when I was high, in the times that I was planning on getting high, when I was working on my next drunk, or trying to get sober so that I could go back out again. It was all about me and my selfishness. At that point in my life I can assure you there was nobody who came into my path who was not damaged by my behaviors—hurt by my words, deeds, thought processes, profane language, etc.

How long is your list? Don't make a short list and pretend that it doesn't matter because this is really the turning point in breaking the cycle of focusing on what you want and beginning to focus on what is in the best interest of others. I talked about willingness. It is an action word that becomes an act of your free will. It is about opportunity and how you are going to make a willing choice to make amends to them all. And remember that at this point who you ever make reparation with does not exist because if you are only looking at a list. Keep in mind that right is right and wrong is wrong. I don't care what your circumstances were at the time, whether you were in prison or somebody else did something to you first.

There may be people that you did prison time with that you need to put on the list, just as there may be people who attend your church that you need to address because you didn't act appropriately at one time or another during a service. How do I know this? I am a minister, and I have seen many people who have come to church that didn't really want to be there. They were trying to accommodate somebody else and they acted like an idiot.

If you got up and left in the middle of a pastor's sermon, put him or her on the list. If you lied to the income tax man, put him on there. When the credit card company that got you to run up $8,000 in credit card debt and then charged you 28 percent interest called you up and tried to collect that claim and you didn't want to pay the money, put it on the list. The guy who you threw the beer bottle at who was mowing the lawn one Saturday morning when you had a hangover, put him on the list too!

You also need to go back and look at old places where you lived in your life. All those old landlords you ran out on or trashed their property, they go on the list. All the people that you married or were shacking up with, you can't skip them either. It also includes all of the people who you had one-night stands with and never called again. Every time you went out to eat and you stiffed the waitress for a tip, you need to add it to the tally. Do you grasp the extent of what I'm talking about yet?

This is damage assessment. Moreover, it is about a change of lifestyle. It is not making an apology. An "I'm really sorry that I screwed up your entire life and now you are in shambles", will never be sufficient. Look at this more along the lines of: "I am here because I have been screwed up my whole life and now I'm working on trying to change. I have damaged you way beyond anything I could imagine, and I am here to produce an opportunity for you and I to correct what we can. What do I need to do to make this right?" This process is about starting to look at cleaning up your side of the street and restoring dignity to all those you have wronged. In doing so, you bring dignity to yourself.

This process is where you begin to reach out and love other people, where you become accountable for your actions of past, present, and future. It is where the shame issue gets addressed because you cannot express love while emotionally rooted in shame. Most addicts grew up in shame factories; they grew up being ashamed of everything. You might not have done well in school and your parents said you should be ashamed of yourself. They were speaking shame into your life.

Shame at the dinner table was one of my big issues. My parents would place too much food on the plate and then say, "You need to eat everything. Don't you know there are starving children all over the world?" Now I have more than I can possibly eat as a kid with an order of guilt on the side. There is no wonder why we have food maladies in our generation. It's because we produced them back in the childhood years in our shame factories. This step is the place where you can cut yourself free from this emotional trap and turn off the shame switch.

Gaining humility helps to begin the process of removing shame, which is rooted in deep in our core. Shame is all about you. You were shamed by other people, or you were shamed by your own behaviors. When you break this cycle you learn that you can either love or hurt each person that you encounter. When you decide that you no longer want to hurt other people you are on the path of embracing the principle of brotherly love.

I remember when I told my sponsor that I was praying to help people at night. He said that was great, but before I did that I should pray that I don't hurt people. Hurt people will always hurt people. I was still hurt and needed healing before I could help anyone, I needed help. Wounded people wound other people. There is a thin line between carrying the message and carrying the mess and between carrying the cure and spreading the disease. In early recovery people tend to teeter on these edges, so it's important to remember that every day you carry the potential to either love or hurt someone.

You cannot love anyone without liking them first. You can use that nonsense line, "Well I love everybody, but I don't like them all." It's just not true. Liking precedes loving, so you have to practice learning how to like people. Sow some seeds of kindness towards others. Smile at people and say something nice. It's that simple. Start practicing because if you sow those seeds you will begin to reap a harvest back. To love you is a good thing, but to love others is even better. For this to work you need to understand unconditional love. This is the type of love that doesn't have attachments or require anything back. If you only love the people that love you back there is no merit. Some people have been sowing bad into relationships for so long that they just keep reaping wave after wave of negative in return. You reap what you sow, always. If you fall into this negative reaping category, I would recommend that you pray for a crop failure and start over again!

To start planting new seeds, you need to understand what love truly is. Here are some dimensions of what love encompasses:

- **Love puts up with many faults.** In a family that has love, individual desires always will be compromised and give and take will rule. This includes some dimensions of personal suffering. Without that ebb and flow, choices are eliminated and love gives way to rigidity.

- **Love is kind.** When you are kind you are useful to other people. There was a bumper sticker I saw some years ago that said, "Practice random acts of kindness." This gives an indication that there are many opportunities in the course of the day to be genuinely kind. Doing something for someone else that is not a requirement demonstrates true human caring. I don't know about random acts out of the gate in recovery, but at least you should be moving in the right direction by being kind to those closest to you in life. Just be nice!

- **Love does not envy.** That means there is no jealousy in love and you do not covet what another has when you love him or her. The thing that I envied the most when I first got sober was people that had many years in recovery. It bothered me because they would get up in meetings and say things that made sense. Then I found something out. When I had that many years I was old and had grey hair, and I found out that wrinkles don't hurt. Now I am no longer jealous.

  On the flip side, I remember there was a guy who was around for a long time when I first got sober. He would chair the meeting and say, "Well I have been sober 48 years…since I have been sober 48 years I have learned a few things about being sober 48 years." It was in every sentence: 48 years, 48 years, 48 years. Nobody needs to brag about something like this because you only have today.

- **Love is not proud.** The key negative component of pride is not being teachable. If you cannot learn you are not walking in love and you need to change that.

- **Love is not perverse.** Do I need to go further? Sex and love are not the same thing! When you go to a strip club you are not going to find love. Many failed relationships were founded on this misunderstanding.

- **Love is not selfish, and it is not easily provoked.** If you have a short fuse and you go off the handle all the time, you are not living in a state of love. Instead, you are living in a state of anger, and angry people cannot be in the spirit and consciousness of love. They may still feel the emotion in passing, but they have not attained love's core state of existence, which is an expression of giving and kindness.

- **Love thinks no wrong.** When you love people you don't conjure up bad thoughts about them. Thoughts create emotions, and emotions have energy. Therefore, bad thoughts will create negative energy that can be unknowingly projected on others. The man who envisions his wife cheating on him will find the thoughts creating the abstract emotion called jealousy. The negative energy will often manifest in aggressive anger and even violence if not checked.

- **Love doesn't celebrate other people's failures.** Don't say things after the fact like, "Well I knew he was going to relapse." If you knew he was going to relapse, then you should have told him that you thought he was going to relapse and tried to help him.

- **Love celebrates things that are honest.** The great expression of unconditional love found in recovery meetings is often displayed in the celebration of honesty, particularly when someone comes clean about a recent failure or episode of "stinkin - thinking" Groups of supporters will speak out and even applaud at this honesty. This is such a wonderful manifestation of true brotherly love.

There are three other things that love embodies. Love is trusting, which we discussed early in the chapter; love hopes for the best; and love hangs in there. You are not in recovery because of your own best thinking, so I want to close this chapter with a visualization that I call the field of suffering.

"One day I was walking along through life and suddenly I found myself in the field of suffering. I don't know how I got there exactly, but I was standing in the middle of this field and it was nothing by briars and stickers and stones and hard places. There wasn't anything good that I could see. This field could be a divorce, loss of a friend to death, sickness, a financial loss; you can add your own idea there.

I have been through many of these, you may have been too. This field is a place where you feel all alone and everything is barren. You are standing there, and you don't know what to do so you just start walking. You begin to put one foot in front of the other, you walk forward and finally you come out on the edge of the field and you look at yourself and you are all bruised, scratched, and torn up. But at least you have finished the journey. Then as you go through life you keep look-ing back at the field and wondering, "Why did I have to go through that and experience the pain?" As a result you are always puzzled al-ways filled with regret and sorrow.

But if you will to go back there for a minute and take a look in the middle of the field of suffering where nothing good seems to grow; look around and you will find that there is one lone flower growing there. You will find it nowhere else in the universe. It's a flower that only grows in the middle of suffering, it's called the flower compassion. Now take a moment to bend down and pick that flower and carry it with you. Now walk out to the edge of the field and brush off the bram-bles, put some ointment on the scratches and bruises. As you move away from the Field of Suffering you will always have a reason for the journey. Hold that flower close to your heart. You will never have to look back again and wonder why you went through the pain; it is the place you have found the greatest treasure in the universe, compassion for others. When you walk with that compassion you become a help to those who are in the same predicament.

You probably have been through the field many times. You have been divorced more than once, or maybe you have been locked up in more than one state. You went bankruptcy and lost everything. You had your children taken away from you. You had close friends who died and you thought you were going to be next. Go back to one of those fields, search out and pick the flower of compassion. A person who has been through many fields and learns to collect all those flow-ers then walks with a bouquet that gives off the aroma called compas-sion, and the greatest demonstration of brotherly love is a person able to be moved with compassion.

The greatest of these is love - - -

There were two boys who grew up in Catholic school together, Anthony Sicola and Timothy O'Leary. They were best friends, but it was known that Anthony Sicola was just a cut above Timothy O'Leary, just a little better at everything. After finishing high school, they both felt the call to go into the priesthood, and they went to college and then seminary to begin studies. It was not very long before it was obvious that Anthony Sicola had an edge over Timothy O'Leary.

The day came when they graduated. They were both ordained as priests, went on assignments, and later they both were recommended to become Bishops. All the while, Anthony Sicola did just a little better in fulfilling his duties. He was more connected in the communities he served , and he reached out just a hair further than Timothy O'Leary. Then they both were selected to become Cardinals, and Anthony Sicola was just a little more politically astute than Timothy O'Leary.

He was better at raising funds, and he had more organizations under his jurisdiction.

It soon was seen throughout the Catholic world that Anthony Sicola probably would be named the next Pope. Many years went by and when the Pope passed away both Anthony Sicola and Timothy O'Leary were candidates to succeed him. The selection process began, and it wasn't very long until the white smoke came up out of the chimney indicating that the Cardinals had come to a decision. It was Timothy O'Leary.

Needless to say, Anthony Sicola was upset. He knew he always stood out above Timothy O'Leary, so he commanded an audience with all the Cardinals. "Everybody knows that I was next in line to be Pope, and I want an answer as to why you didn't select me," he said.

It was quiet and finally this little old Italian Cardinal stood up and he said in broken English, "Antony, you akno tha we a lova you, and we a know that youda makeada better pope, but Antony wea gotta ona problem, Antony, if wea makada you the pope you woulda bea forever known as the "Pope Sicola."

CHAPTER 9

DISCIPLINE

When I got sober, I had a job making $135 a week and all I could steal. Believe me, I took a whole lot more than I made. It was a uniform company that sold many other products, such as shop towels and factory supplies. On my route, I memorized all the stops where people were likely to leave money in their uniform pockets, and I could go through those clothes so fast that it would make your head spin. And that wasn't all I pilfered. I had a basement full of towels and enough fender covers to supply a manufacturing plant. I had about 40 pairs of pants in my size. They were all the same color. I had enough short-sleeved shirts to wear until I retired, and they all said Dave on them. I don't even like being called Dave rather than David! I had taken stuff I didn't need and couldn't use in a lifetime.

When it was time to make right the wrong, my sponsor helped me out. He was a nice guy concerned about me doing prison time, so we went to a restaurant and used a public payphone to call that company. He made the call, and it was comical. He was trying to explain to my former boss on the other end of the line that he was sponsoring a guy who used to work for him.

"He stole a bunch of junk and he is finally sober and he wants to bring it all back."

My old boss said, "Well we need his social security number and we'll have to prosecute…"

Click! My sponsor hung up the phone.

We had to figure out another plan. He said, "How did you get this stuff?" I said I stole it. So he said take it back the same way you stole. I was petrified I might get caught, but I loaded up my trunk and back-seat anyway. You could hardly see out the windows and I was sneaking down to the plant like Secret Agent Man. I knew the gate wasn't locked after the day shift because there was an 11:00 pm truck that came in. I watched the last guy leave as I was sitting in my car sweating and smoking Marlboros two at a time. Then I opened that gate and drove my car out behind the building as fast as I could. I was in such a hurry I wacked my head getting out of the car. At first I was going to stack this stuff along the side of the building, but in a few minutes I was throwing it.

When I was done I drove straight to a meeting. It was the first time in my life I have ever had a migraine, and I was soaked with sweat. People kept asking me if I had relapsed. I asked my sponsor what to do next, and he said one day God will bring your old boss into your path so you can make an amends to him.

A few months later, I finally borrowed a car and I talked a woman into going out on a date. I took her to a nice restaurant at the mall. We made a reservation and the hostess gave us a beeper so we could walk around the shops until our table was ready. So we are walking along and I looked up and here comes my former boss from the uniform company. I thought, now the Lord couldn't be arranging that—not to-night, on a date.

He saw me and said, "Hey, how are you doing?"

So I'm standing in front of this guy and I know I have got to make amends to him. He is talking on and on, and she is standing there look-ing at me with a look that says, "Why are we standing here forever?"

So finally I said to him, "I need to tell you something. You remem-ber some time ago there was an employee that stole a bunch of stuff from the company that wanted to return it?"

He just looked at me and said, "That was you wasn't it?"

"Yeah," I said, "I just wanted to mention that and straighten it out".

He said, "Don't worry about it," and then he went right back to talking like nothing had happened. He went on his way, and we went on our way, which turned out to be back to the car because she wanted to go home. We never went out again. Two weeks later, I got word the man passed away. That was the only time that I would have been able to make that reparation, and that is why God put us together at that specific time and place.

> **Step 9:** *Made direct amends to such people wherever possible, except when to do so would injure them or others.*

⚷ PRINCIPLE: DISCIPLINE

When correcting your behavior that caused damage to others, like we discussed in Chapter 8, it is not about you, it's about others. It's about making the restitution no matter what or how bad the circumstances. You very well might have something radical to straighten out in your life, and if you avoid doing it by skipping this process it will become your biggest enemy. What you don't correct will always cause you to fall back into your old patterns of behavior. What you don't destroy will eventually destroy you.

This is about finding those people wherever and whenever you can and openly and honestly righting the damage done by you. When you do this be sure that further damage doesn't occur to anyone. You have a list of all the people that you have injured and become *willing* to go to them, everyone and get things right. And while you don't actually end up going to everybody, going back to straighten out as many wrongs as possible without hurting others is an imperative if you are ever going to get whole and get well.

In order to complete this process you are going to have to understand the principle of discipline, which is always a prerequisite to change. If your actions are going to mean something in your life, you must change. You may connect the idea of discipline to your childhood, where it was punishment for doing wrong or not doing right. However, there is a big difference between punishment and discipline. Punishment is a deterrent from wrong, but it does nothing to address how to improve and what needs to be done to make lasting changes.

Most involved in recovery want to see big changes, and they want to see them immediately. They are undisciplined in their lifestyles and this carries over into the recovery process. In contrast, those who have experienced the discipline of sports, getting into shape, the rigors of military training, or college study, know that doing small things frequently will result in big changes and accomplishments over time. With diligence to performing smaller amends, you will learn and experience great results long term. The following list will help you understand exactly what this entails:

- Discipline is a process of doing the next right thing.

- Discipline is doing the right small things.

- Discipline is what you do right in your life that causes you to change for the better.

- Discipline means clarity and focus on a certain problem.

- Discipline is a formation of good habits that produce positive results.

- Discipline requires hard work and attention to thoughts, words, and actions.

- Discipline reflects loyalty and faith. (Undisciplined lifestyles reflect laziness and bad habits.)

- Discipline is balance, not perfection.

- Discipline requires confronting incorrect lifestyle choices.

- Discipline starts with duty.

- Discipline moves from duty to desire.

- Discipline moves actions from desire to delight.

- Discipline of a spiritual nature is a clear pathway to get to know God and do His will.

- Discipline is about delighting in doing God's will.

- Discipline shapes your life into a new path.

- Discipline produces devotion to a healthy, peaceful life.

Now that you know what creates the foundation of discipline, you need to understand that the inability to forgive is the major stumbling to repairing those who were damaged. Unforgiveness will stop you from moving forward past this point in the recovery process. If you are like most people, you are unwilling to make corrections with others because you have not forgiven people for what they have done to you. And, at the same time, you are pretty sure that they have not forgiven you for what you have done to them. This is what you say in your mind: I'm not going to forgive them until they change. And they are looking at you saying he (or she) is never going to change so why should I forgive him (or her). Neither side wants to give in, so it's going to require yet another secondary principle called charity in order to break that cycle.

Somebody has to get off square one to straighten the mess out and you are that somebody! Right now you are probably thinking, "Why do I have to forgive them? They haven't forgiven me? Why do I have to be the one?" It's because you are the one that decided that you didn't want to die drunk or from a drug overdose. Aren't you the one that decided to enter the recovery process so that you didn't have to spend the rest of your life in prison, jail, the insane asylum, or in the gutter on the side of the street? Aren't you the one that wants to get better? If so, you have to start this whole deal. The other people may never get better. Quite often, they are just as sick as you were when you entered into recovery. Most likely, you would like them to get better so that you can forgive them, but I can assure you that many of them will never get better.

If you were married to somebody and the very sound of his or her name sends shivers through your spine and your hair stands up on the top of your head, you probably lack forgiveness. If hearing the name of the father or mother of your children drives you to thoughts of homicide immediately, you definitely need to work on forgiveness! It doesn't matter who started the battle. It's the one who ends it who is smart.

Matthew 5:9 says, *"Blessed are the peacemakers for they shall be called the children of God."* We all want to be know as the children of God, so the beginning of this is to make peace. To make peace you must forgive, period.

To forgive (for-give) means to give in advance. Like forbearance, to put up with in advance; foregone conclusion, again in advance, foreclosure, closing in advance; to forgive is to give in advance of any changes. You decide in advance not to hold whatever it was to someone's account anymore. I'm not going to hold that person responsible any longer. If I decide to forgive you for something, it simply means that I am going to release you from the perceived obligation I believe you have to me. You owed me something and I felt entitled to it. When I forgive somebody he or she no longer owes me anything, not even an apology. It's done.

You may go into this forgiveness thing saying, "Let me decide what I can say that has worked in the past to get someone to forgive me." You are like a skilled craftsman when it comes to words, and you put them together when you want something. You are slick, and you believe you can smooth your way out of any situation. You know how to use words to endear a person to you. You are an expert at drawing on their emotions and spinning situations around.

This is called manipulation, and it won't work for two reasons. First, it's a short-term solution, a temporary fix for a permanent problem. And when the temporary fix wears off and the real you shows up, you are going to be in a worse position than you were before. Why? Because now not only did that person not believe you when you were drinking or using drugs, he or she doesn't believe you when you are clean and sober.

You want people to forgive you. It's natural, normal, and healthy to desire this. Maybe you want forgiveness from your wife because you went out and cheated on her. Or maybe you want your son to forgive you because you didn't show up for his Little League game and he hit a home run while you were in Joe's Tavern sucking down a beer. You want your boss to forgive you because you stole money from the company. You want everybody to forgive you so you try to manipulate them into liking you again. The problem is that if you have this attitude it reflects self-centeredness, self-seeking, and self-will run riot, and it stems from low self esteem and low self worth. If this is where you are at, you need to drop back to Chapter 4 and figure out the real problem.

Here's the secret: Forgive other people and to the same measure that you have forgiven them you will be forgiven. Most people try to access forgiveness from people before they access forgiveness from God, and you can't truly embrace forgiveness from God until you learn how to forgive *other* people. In other words, my ability to receive forgiveness from God—and reach that place where I am no longer walking in guilt or shame—is directly linked to my willingness to forgive other people. My ability to receive forgiveness from God postures me in faith, because now I understand what forgiveness is, and that enhances and establishes my ability to receive forgiveness from other people.

If you became willing to identify those you harmed, you now have the potential and know how to forgive other people. Remember you said you were willing to make it right with them all. You made a decision on the inside that nobody owes you anything. When I got into the position where I felt as if nobody owed me anything, I decided that nobody ever is going to owe me anything again. How does that work? First, I don't cosign for anybody and secondly I only lend money to people if I can afford to give it to them, and then I don't expect them to ever give it back. Interestingly they usually don't.

On the flip side of the coin, let me give you some things that forgiveness *is not*:

Forgiveness is not a requirement of life. You can live in this life without forgiveness, but you can never be free until you forgive. Many find it possible to live with pockets of "unforgivness" in their hearts. As a result, they stay sober but they are never totally free. There is always a shadow of some sort hanging over their heads. I have found in my observations that they believe they are free, but they have never tasted true freedom.

Forgiveness is not agreeing with the perpetrator. If you got robbed by a man you may decide to forgive him, but that doesn't mean you are agreeing with the act. It just means that you are not going to hold it to his account. Do you know why? It's because if you hold it to his account you are still emotionally attached to him. Have you ever noticed that when you don't forgive somebody you are still connected to that person? There is a connection from your soul to their soul.

Forgiveness allows you to cut the ties.

Forgiveness is not underwriting the behavior or cosigning the wrong. If you choose to forgive it is never an endorsement of wrong doing. Forgiveness requires releasing the other person from your judgment, but it does not bring with it a need to adjust your personal standards of right and wrong.

Forgiveness is not surrendering to abuse—past, present, or future. When the police officer comes to the house for domestic violence and you are all black and blue while the other person is sitting over in the corner sucking a beer, it's time to prosecute. Not filing charges is not forgiveness, it's stupidity. That is codependency, which also is an addiction and a sickness.

Forgiveness is not dismissal of responsibility. You may forgive people, but that doesn't dismiss their responsibilities. For example, it might be to the legal system for child support. Your forgiveness doesn't free others from the judge's rule. I forgave my son, and he still went to prison. It didn't dismiss him from his responsibility to the law for crimes he committed.

Forgiveness is not righting the wrong. It is deciding not to hold somebody accountable for something he or she did. Remember, to forgive is to give in advance. It is similar to forbear, a foregone conclusion, or to foreclose. They all assume action of some sort in advance. As a result, in advance of the wrong being righted you give the person in question the gift of release from any obligation to you regarding the matter.

Forgiveness is not forgetting, although that is the goal. Some people understand how to forgive, but not how to forgive and forget. Let me help you understand something: Your memories are your memories forever. You have neural pathways that are created by experiences in life, and when you have trauma there is negative imprinting within your brain. It can be measured scientifically, and it does not go away. However, there is something that goes away when you forgive—and that is the pain associated with the memory.

Forgiveness is not trust, which might never be reestablished or perhaps never should be. If somebody stole money from you every time you left your wallet out you can forgive him or her, but if you still leave your wallet out and trust that person you are not very smart. One thing I have learned in life is that evil is predictable. Liars lie, thieves steal, and cheaters cheat. Because you decide to forgive someone doesn't mean he or she has stopped the negative behavior.

Forgiveness is not vengeance or settling the score. Have you ever felt like you wanted to get even with someone at one time in your life? Before I entered into recovery I never wanted to get even, I wanted to get extra. I wanted everything you owed me, and then I wanted more. I wanted to make you pay for the wrong you did to me. I wanted it back with interest.

Overall, forgiveness is a process, not an event, and when you enter into the process there are specific steps you must take. Many try to forgive and fall short because they believe it is a simple choice. To find the path to forgive I suggest you do the following five things:

You must own the pain. If you can feel it, God can heal it. People often want to mask pain and pretend it doesn't exist. They get pills out of the medicine cabinet or pour a few strong drinks, and before they know it they are addicted.

Identify the specific hurt: who, what, where, and when. Don't be fooled by the old expression that time heals all wounds. Time makes it fade, but fading is different than healing. Fading means that I am not thinking about it right now. But bring it up again and see just how well it healed. Moreover, if time heals, God is not necessary.

Communicate your forgiveness to another person. Make sure it's someone who is not involved emotionally. This is similar to Chapter 5, where you confessed to God, acknowledged to yourself, and shared with somebody your deep secrets.

Communicate your forgiveness to the one who wronged you if appropriate. You need to tell the person who hurt you that you forgive him or her. Maybe you need to do it through a letter or through a sponsor, or maybe through a judge. Just remember this lesson on forgiveness does not preempt restraining orders!

Forget about the matter or at least refuse to discuss it beyond forgiving someone. Do you know why forgiveness doesn't work for most people? It's because they chose to forgive, they enter into that process, and then all they talk about is the hurt and pain. They rehearse it to every person that they meet. They go on and on and on and on. You need to change what is coming out of your mouth after you forgive someone. Stop bringing the issue up!

When you bury something that is dead, you don't want to dig it up again and smell it. If you do you will enter into self pity and feel sorry for yourself and that will lead to bitterness, antipathy and offence. The main reason that people relapse back into their addictions is they begin to mentally dig up old sour feelings. They become filled with dissatisfaction on the inside touchy and agitated and begin to seek relief.

As soon as you forgive somebody that you didn't have to forgive, you have entered into one of the most sublime pleasures of life. It is one of the greatest things that could ever happen: You have won. You won! You have been competing throughout your entire life trying to win at everything and anything, and finally you have done it. And now you find out that you never have to compete with anyone ever again. The battle is over.

You can't make these repairs to everybody because it's not in some cases appropriate, but when you enter into the forgiveness process you will begin to understand who you can approach and who you cannot face head on. I don't recommend that you go back and make amends to your wife and your children right away. Start with somebody that doesn't matter much as much in the grand scheme of your life, like Billy Bob down at the tire and lube who you stole a ratchet from 15 years ago. He might take his other ratchet and whack you with it, but if you mess up the forgiveness and reparation process it will not have a long-term negative impact on your life going forward.

However, if you screw up the amends to your wife - - - the state you live in probably still has alimony! Make sure you get that one right. Listen, you don't want to go back to your family and cause more harm than good. You only have one mother and one father, and if they are still alive you probably are walking on thin ice when it comes to re-pairing the damage you have done to your relationship with them. If you have children they probably have been through a lot, so don't take chances by approaching them if you are not truly ready. Practice on people who are less significant in your life.

If you relapsed half a dozen times, try starting your amends with your past sponsors, or go back down to the convenience store where you stole a six pack every day for two months and pay the money back. Discipline is necessary in this process because it requires that you do difficult things that you would rather avoid. And you have to start small and work toward larger goals. It's like exercising. You don't start out running a marathon when you haven't jogged in 10 years. You need to build up to the big race.

Discipline is where you do a little bit at a time until you can mani-fest the desired results. It starts off as drudgery, then it becomes duty, and then it transforms into delight.

This guy named Marty woke up at home with a huge hangover. He forced himself to open his eyes, and the first thing he saw was a couple of aspirins and a glass of water on the side table. Then he looked down and saw his clothing in front of him, all clean and pressed. He looked around the room and saw that it was in perfect order--spotless and clean. So was the rest of the house!

He took the aspirins and noticed a note on the table: "Honey, breakfast is on the stove. I left early to go shopping. Love You!"

So he went to the kitchen and sure enough, there was a hot breakfast and the morning newspaper.

His son was at the table eating. Marty asked him, "Son, what happened last night?"

His son said, "Well Dad, you came home after 3 am drunk and delirious. You broke some furniture, puked in the hallway, and gave yourself a black eye when you stumbled into the door!"

Confused, Marty asked, "So why is everything in order and so clean, with breakfast on the table waiting for me?"

His son replied, "Oh, that! Mom dragged you to the bedroom. When she tried to take your pants off you said, "Lady, leave me alone. I'm married!"

A self-induced hangover - $100.00 - - - Broken furniture - $200.00 - - - Breakfast - $10.00 - - - saying the right thing - "PRICELESS"

CHAPTER 10

PERSEVERANCE

In my early days of sobriety, speaking in front of a group seemed like an impossibility. I would get so nervous I would become physically sick. However, the more I spoke, the more comfortable I became in front of other people. Some years later I entered the ministry and the groups became larger. It seemed as if more was required of me, and once again I became nervous every time I was called to speak.

The old saying "practice makes perfect" kept coming to mind as I progressed along this pathway, and I followed my internal advice and focused my efforts. It paid off because I found that buried under all of that fear was a true God-given gift to present and teach. It started to become natural. As long as I spent time in prayer and study prior to speaking it would go well. As the years of experience compounded, so did my joy of speaking. Those who didn't know my long learning curve and perseverance often would remark how natural and easy I made it look.

Then one day I was talking, and I noticed that I was getting words stuck and even stuttering a little. Over a period of a couple months this progressed until it seemed like I couldn't get a sentence out without stuttering. I was sure that my speaking career was shot, and I didn't know what I would do next. It was even suggested that I go to a neurologist to help find the source of this problem.

One night I was out late walking and praying, trying to make sense of it all, when what I know to be the voice of God spoke in my heart. It said: "You have become reliant on your ability to speak and not on Me." It was one of the clearest messages I ever received from God, and it was absolutely true. I had forgotten where I had come from, and who had graced me to speak in the first place. I repented, to say the least.

The next morning when I woke up 90 percent of the speaking problem was gone. Today, I have no trouble addressing large crowds or remembering who gets the credit for my skill. Occasionally I still stumble over a word, but when it happens I immediately inventory my attitude and reconnect with God. It is an ongoing and daily process that requires diligence and perseverance, but the rewards far outweigh the effort, and my life is now filled with gratitude for the talents God has bestowed in my life.

> **Step 10:** *Continued to take personal inventory and when we were wrong promptly admitted it.*

PRINCIPLE: PERSEVERANCE

I hope by now you realize the need to continue moving forward, and perseverance is the principle that now comes into play. In my experience, I have seen that people who do not stay focused and on track in any recovery program tend to become stagnant, and when this happens they start moving back in the opposite direction—slipping toward their addictions.

They don't even stay constant at a particular point because they become apathetic and complacent, and then they stop doing the things that they learned how to do to maintain a healthy state of sobriety. They no longer register their daily activities. They stop looking at their behaviors, and pretty soon they begin to drift emotionally. The next thing you know they are completely out of touch with recovery and the process of rehabilitating their lives. More importantly, they become isolated from God and removed from the people who care about them. As a result, they decide to pick up alcohol or drugs or even enter another type of addiction not yet tried.

This is where you ensure that this doesn't happen—that you don't become apathetic and lose your focus. It's important to note here that the chief reason for failure known to mankind is broken focus. On the contrary, a man or women with a focus creates a majority. Focus around an objective, such as staying sober is at the core of what we call perserverance. Ask yourself these questions: Do you have a focus on recovery or not? Do you have a focus on getting your life back together or not? Do you have a focus on your spiritual life process or not?

Maintaining a focus is a component of learning how to persevere, and this is part of a continuing process. Remember that you cannot continue something that you have not started. This is the continuation of everything that you have learned so far in recovery.

In Chapter 1 you learned about honesty. Have you continued to be scrupulously honest? Do you still have hope, the principle of Chapter 2? In Chapter 3 faith was addressed. Do you have faith? Have you moved away from that place of superstition, where you have a God of your own fabrication, into the process where you actually have faith to believe that there is an all-knowing, omnipresent God; are you in contact with the God of your experience? If you have made this transition, you turn to the principle of Chapter 4, which is courage. Are you still afraid? Are you still living in fear or have you moved out of fear and acquired some boldness in recovery by recognizing that you are an addict or an alcoholic and that is never going to change?

Let's look at this a little closer. Are you still ashamed about being an alcoholic or an addict? Are you still trying to mask it when you are around people and make up excuses? If you are an alcoholic and somebody offers you a drink, do you say, "I would take it but I would probably get sick," or do you say, "No thanks, I am an alcoholic." Personally, I am no longer ashamed. God has changed that for me. Do I have some regrets? Yes, but I don't live in them anymore. Today I am happy to tell people the things that I have come through. It's not because I think it is wonderful that I became an alcoholic. It is because I am happy that I met God; that He removed the desire I had to drink and He has kept me sober for three decades. That empowers me to help other people.

The next principles in the process we have discussed are courage and integrity. When you have the courage to complete a hard look at the way you were and share it with openness you found integrity and you become a whole person again. Reputation Man and Character Man, those two different personalities embodied in you, actually re-integrate. What you see is what you get. I don't have to pretend today. Do you like yourself? Do you like who you are? I do, and it is one of the benefits of completing this part of the process. Do the following exercise and it will help you understand the feeling I am trying to convey. Look in the mirror for just a minute. There you will see a person, and it's the only one like this in the world. Look at your image and say, "I'm unique. I'm special. I'm me." Tell yourself "I love you". Practice until you are comfortable.

Are you willing? Willingness is the principle of Chapter 6, and perserverance has a strong tie to it and your decision making processes. People will readily tell you about what they are willing to do to recover. However, they usually don't realize that the thing that is going to trip them as they walk through this process is the one thing they are *not* willing to do. To keep from falling, you must learn to walk with humility, the principle of Chapter 7. And this is not groveling and pretending that you are worthless.

We move from humility to brotherly love in Chapter 8. Do you have that love or not? If you do, you are well on your way to begin the process of helping other people and preparing to right the wrongs in your life. The principle of brotherly love and the Chapter 9 principle of discipline both are wrapped within forgiveness. Have you learned to embrace forgiveness? Remember, forgiveness is not an event, it is a process.

In a nutshell, this is the path you have walked to arrive at the principle of perseverance. Here we persistently, consistently work on all that we have done and continue to do. To take individual daily account of who we are and what we are doing, both good and bad. When we enter this process we can face our wrongs acknowledge our failures. This critical step focuses on activating all of these principles into one process in your life that encompasses everything—the good, the bad, and the ugly. This is the place where you have to do the things that you really don't want to do to remain whole.

When I persevere, I put another day between me and my old self. The man that I used to be would pick up a drink and want to fight. I didn't care what I was arguing about, or what side the other person was on. I would take the opposite side and fight. That was not a good characteristic, and I am grateful that I have put it to rest. However, I have to remember that my old self can always show up if I do not deal with all of my issues on a daily basis.

It was explained to me when I first got sober that I needed to set the drink down, turn around, and begin to move a day at a time in the opposite direction. What I had been doing up to this point was placing the drink somewhere out in the future and walking toward it. I needed to make the drink a part of my past, not a part of my future.

If you are wondering where the next drink (or drug) is, it is sitting right alongside of your last drink (or drug). Do you know where you put it? I know where I put the last drink down, and I have been walking away from it for all these years. As a result, I would have to go through a whole tapestry of meetings, prayer groups, recovery books I have read, people I have helped, funerals I have attended, and sermons I have heard to reach that drink. I don't ever want to go back through all of these experiences again. Some of them are good I don't want to damage my accomplishments. Some of them are bad and I don't want to relive them. *If you can't remember where your last drink or drug is at, you probably haven't had it yet.*

Perseverance will help you assimilate all of the other principles and move towards God. If the principles are not part of your life, you are moving in the direction of self, and self is going to fail. Perseverance will keep momentum in your life and ensure that you are taking personal stock of your life every day. If you don't do this daily accounting I can absolutely assure you that your life will drop back into the chaos from which you are emerging. The wreckage of your present is rooted in the wreckage of our past. So be sure if you are engaging in a bad behavior today, it's not old behavior, it is current behavior—and you need to address it quickly.

Perseverance leads you to consistency and puts you in a forward motion toward achieving your goals. Perseverance is not quitting. You need to ask yourself: "What will make me quit? What is it that will make me pick up another drink or drug with the threat of going to jail or losing my family or getting fired from my job?" The top things include:

Over confidence. This is the attitude that says, "I know everything I need to know to stay sober." It is indicative of the person who is not teachable and believes that he or she has heard it all and no longer needs to listen.

Broken focus. This bears repeating: broken focus is one of the top reasons you will return to a state of active addiction. You stop going to meetings, you don't remain in contact with people in recovery and, most importantly, you stop praying.

Self pity. Feeling sorry for yourself. For example, feeling that life is not fair or everyone is out to get you. Self pity will lead to isolation quicker than anything else.

Resentment. If you have a resentment against somebody you have anger toward that person, and the next step is that you will resist him or her. As a result, you may resist somebody that you need in your life. And if you resist that person long enough you will reject him or her. In the end, you may reject the very person that God sent to help you. If you can catch yourself in resentments—before you move into resisting and rejecting—your life will be much better in the long run. Remember the three Rs: **resentment, resistance, and rejecting**.

Now that you understand the feelings and behaviors that can take you back out into your addiction, you can use the inventory on a daily basis to remain objective and the three positive Rs to remove personal resentments. The first R is **reconsider**. You need to reconsider that person and look at him or her the way God does. Then you need to **reconnect** with that person and reopen the lines of communication. Finally, it's time to **reconstruct** the relationship.

From a broader perspective, in this review there are five specific realms that must be explored:

Physical. A lot of recovering addicts' depression, confusion, and sleepless nights come from a failure to inventory their physical condition. You need to look at nutrition and exercise. Consider how much caffeine and sugar you are consuming, for example, and evaluate the other types of foods you eat.

Mental. Take a look at any crazy mental gymnastics that you are doing in your head. You need to learn how to inventory your thought processes. There is a whole variety of things that you should consider including truth, the purity of your thoughts, your rapport with others, and the virtue of your behaviors. If you neglect to pay attention to what you are thinking, your mind will be negatively impacted by outside stimulus. Don't let the crazy thoughts take charge, and you should not believe everything that you think! In fact, most of it is not true. Most of what you think is based on your experience, and if you are an addict or an alcoholic most of your experience probably has been bad.

Relational. Your life is an accumulation of relationships. The main thing that is going to impact your future is the people that you meet and your sources of information and learning. Take a good look at the people who surround you on a daily basis. You will attract people to you who are like you. Are you attracting intelligent, kind people or are you attracting crazy people?

When I first entered into recovery I attracted nothing but crazy people. I went and complained to my sponsor. I said everybody in recovery is crazy. He said, "No it's just the ones who are around you." If you do what is right, what is wrong and who is wrong will exit your life. And what is right and who is right will enter your life. There are people coming and going all the time.

Emotional. You are not defined by what you feel, you are defined by what you believe. I now believe that what I believe makes me who I am. An inventory of your emotions will clarify the areas in which you are allowing those emotions to dictate your decisions. Identifying what you feel allows you to adjust thoughts and beliefs, and stay away from the dangerous emotions that produce poor choices.

Spiritual. When you develop a spiritual connection it also becomes a part of your ongoing inventory. You are wrong if you have the belief, "It doesn't matter what I do because I am not hurting anybody but me." When you do the wrong things it affects everybody in your life, and the recovery process revolves around developing your spiritual life. Are you where you need to be right now on the spiritual front? It's not very complicated; just ask yourself, "Did I spend a sufficient amount of time in prayer today?"

The best thing you can do in your life to produce lasting change and avoid returning to your addiction is to take an account every day. Recovery is not so much about beginning well as finishing well. It is a lifetime commitment. Without inventorying your life on a daily basis, you probably will become part of the statistics of those who were in the recovery rooms but then disappeared without a trace.

To make daily changes and improvements in your life, you need to become diligent and do reviews. You cannot change what you are not willing to confront, and you will never control what you are willing to tolerate. It has been proven that there is a genetic predisposition for alcoholism and drug addiction. Do you want to end it in your generation or do you want it to continue on to your sons and your daughters and your grandchildren? If you want it to end you can do something to break that cycle: stop overlooking the little things that eventually will grow into major character and behavior flaws down the road. Change your life and stop making bad choices. It's not all about you! And remember you will never go out on a bender by yourself. Everyone in your life is along with you for the ride in some way.

When a winner makes a mistake, he admits he is wrong. When the loser makes a mistake he gives excuses. Those negative things in your life that you fail to destroy will come back to destroy you. What is the one thing that you are skipping when you take your daily inventory? That is the thing that will come back to haunt you. Your decisions today are going to impact you mentally, emotionally, physically, and spiritually, as well have an effect on your relationships with others and God.

Knowledge by itself will not transform your life. Transformation requires God's power. Your passions and affections are found on the inside and when they are directed at the wrong things they will destroy you. Some people believe knowledge is power, but frequently these individuals are weak and have ineffective knowledge. They might know all about one thing, yet they can't keep a job and they keep getting drunk or using. And we all probably have encountered people who are know-it-alls—they can quote the *Bible* verbatim but they have no actual power in their life to stay away from the first drink and consequently experience relapse after relapse.

Moving knowledge from your head into your heart is really about perseverance. People who get complacent don't stay in recovery. To persevere is to go to meetings, make the phone calls, step on the track and run the lap. Persevere when everything is upside down. If conditions are difficult and you feel the craving remember the saying "this too shall pass." The craving will only last 30 seconds. Persevere through it. Pick up one of the tools of recovery, not the drink or drug. With perseverance you get consistency. With consistency, you build momentum. With momentum, you get achievement. And with achievement, you get the life for which you have been searching.

A duck walked into a bar, waddled over to a stool, jumped up, and then got up on the bar and walked down it. He looked at the bartender. And the bartender looked at him.

The duck said, "Do you have any macadamia nuts?"

The bartender said, "No we don't have macadamia nuts, and we don't allow ducks in here. Get out."

So out the door he went. Then the next day the duck walked back into the bar. Again, he jumped up on the stool, got up on the bar, and walked down toward the bartender.

He asked: "Do you have any macadamia nuts?"

The bartender said, "No we don't have macadamia nuts, and I told you yesterday we don't allow ducks in here. Now get out!"

Quack, quack, quack. Out of the bar he went. So the next day the duck walked in the bar, got up on the stool, jumped up on the bar, and waddled down it. The bartender looked at him with a mean expression.

"Got any macadamia nuts?" the duck asked.

The bartender said, "No, for the last time we don't have macadamia nuts, and if you come in here one more time and ask for macadamia nuts I'm going to nail your web feet to the bar."

Quack, quack, quack, and out the door he went. The next day the duck walked back into the bar again. He jumped up on the stool, and then on the bar. He waddled down the bar. He looked at the bartender and the bartender looked at him.

"Got any nails?" asked the duck.

"No," said the bartender.

"Got any macadamia nuts?"

CHAPTER 11

AWARENESS OF GOD

One time I was at a conference in Baltimore, Md., traveling with a business associate named John. We were staying at a nice hotel on the waterfront, and one of the things the concierge told us when we got out of the cab was not to leave the immediate two or three block area of the hotel. If we did, he added, we probably would not return safely from the surrounding ghetto.

That night my associate and I decided we were going to find something to eat, so we set out from the hotel on foot. It was a cold night and after a while we realized there weren't many streetlights and plenty of burned out cars. We kept walking and then turned a corner—and we saw nothing but endless, deserted streets. Now we had been going quite a while and, needless to say, we were somewhat lost. As we continued along I caught a glimpse of a man walking down the other side of the street near us. I then began watching the reflections in the windows on our side of the street, and I could see that some of his friends were walking along behind us. As a matter of fact, there was a whole gang of guys following us!

I said to John, "I don't want you to look back but I want you to start walking a little bit faster."

He said, "Why?"

"Because we are being followed."

We kept going until we found a fast-food restaurant, and we went inside. The gang quickly showed up in front of the building.

John said, "Let's get a cup of coffee and maybe they will go away."

By the time we got the coffee there were about 15 gang members outside of the window. I went in the bathroom and I said out loud, "Lord, I don't know what to do."

God said, "Go out there and grab John by the hand, pray, and then walk out the side door. I will be with you." This was a little problem in that John was certainly not a guy given to prayer of any kind, especially in public!

I didn't have another plan so I did it. I left the bathroom, found John, and said, "Give me your hands. Reluctantly John conceded. " I prayed right out loud: "Lord, we need your protection. We are going to walk out that side door, and I believe you are going to be with us, and we are going to be fine tonight."

Then I turned to John and said, "Are you ready to go?"

He said no, but we walked out that side door anyway and down the street, and we never saw those guys again. I think they were still standing there, and God steamed up the windows so they couldn't see us leave. John never said much about it when we got back to the hotel and went our separate ways. The next day at the conference I saw John talking to some executives and I walked up and overheard him saying, "...and then David prayed and right after that every-thing changed. We walked out and we were safe!"

The faith I have in God I have because it has been put to the test. Faith that is not tested out may not be faith at all. I am never afraid or embarrassed to pray to God, regardless of the situation, and He always answers me and supports me when I am in need. He can do the same for you.

> **Step 11:** *Sought through prayer and meditation to improve our conscious contact with God as we understood Him, praying only for knowledge of His will for us and the power to carry that out.*

⚷ PRINCIPLE: AWARENESS OF GOD

The principle is awareness of God, and if you have successfully adapted the first 10 principles you should now have some kind of continuous connection with God. You know that somehow there is divine intervention that has come into your life to help you change. This probably is a huge revelation because most likely you have tried to change in the past by exercising your own free will. You attempted to improve your life by willing that you were not going to drink or use anymore—and it never worked.

Does this story sound familiar? You got up in the morning, you were hung over, sick, and broke, and you couldn't remember where you were last night. Maybe you said to yourself, "I swear I'm never going to drink again." By noon you weren't feeling quite so bad. And then by two or three in the afternoon somebody said, "We are stopping on the way home after work. Do you want to have a drink?"

You were on the upswing, and you were thinking maybe you could have one or two drinks and then go home and mow the lawn and do other things that normal people do. So finally five o'clock rolled around and you headed to the bar or the lounge. You went to that place to have one, and you knew you lied to yourself before you even started because you never stopped at one, ever.

Face it: If you are an addict or alcoholic, your willpower doesn't do you much good. Your own free will is what got you into problems. The best plan that you came up with for your life landed you in need of a recovery program. You were doing what you wanted to do, and it started destroying your life.

The connection you make with God will help you break free from this pattern of behavior through prayer and meditation. They are the methods by which you improve your active communication with God and find guidance. Prayer is talking to God, and meditation is calming the mind and clearing it of runaway thoughts and ideas so that the heart is quiet and can hear the voice of God. Personally, I take meditation one step further by clearing extraneous thoughts and then focusing on those things that will enhance my prayer life. However, in order to enhance something you must already have it in place. This is not an unconscious contact with God. This is not some kind of theory or concept that you tap into when things are going bad. This is a conscious awareness that God is in your life and God is activated through your life so you can touch other people.

Contrary to popular belief, you don't have to go to church or to a meeting to find God. You can seek Him anywhere. I talk to God every day, and God talks to me. He doesn't speak to me in King James English, and he doesn't yell at me. As a result of my practice, I have spent more time with God than I have with any living person. Does that make me some kind of spiritual saint? No. It makes me increasingly aware that there is a great need for God in my life.

It is time to identify the patterns that are running in your brain on a daily basis. This is important because you become what you think. If your prayer and meditation practices are rooted entirely in worry and fear, you will not reap the true benefits of these disciplines. To succeed, you need to focus on the things that produce faith rather than those that promote doubt and disbelief. A true daily connection to God makes this possible.

Personally, I have found that God isn't around me. He is in me, through me, and with me all the time. I have an awareness of God when I sit down in a counseling session and somebody begins to open his or her heart and pour it out. I am not sure what to say all the time, but I know that if I listen to that inner voice then I will know what words to speak through God. By the time that person gets up and leaves my office he or she may think I'm brilliant. However, I know that without the guidance of God I would have sunk that conversation.

Many people have knowledge of God, but that's not enough. You need to have contact with Him. It's not as roomy, inclusive, lofty, or poetic as you might think. Let me back up to explain. If you are in the process of building your prayer life and you still are referring to God as some higher power, I can assure that you don't have much understanding of God. If you are in this place you need to go back to Chapter 3 and figure out who God is. I suppose that what you are trying to avoid is restrictions and limitations to your life; if you are in this place, but you can't avoid God for ever.

I certainly didn't want to talk about God when I got sober. I didn't want you to talk about God, and I didn't want to know anything about God because I could not understand Him. At that time, I thought most of the people I met who said they knew something about God were weird! They were the people who came and banged on my door on Saturday morning when I was still hung over, or still drunk. Sometimes I hadn't even been to bed and the Bible thumpers would show up. Or somebody else would come around to tell me all about how Jesus loves me. In my own time I had to come to the conclusion that I could make a connection with God and that I could understand Him as I progressed in recovery.

There has never been anyone who knew anything that would say, find a God that you don't understand and stay that way. It's a God that you can know and begin to understand, and it's the God of your experience. Now is the time to address your conscious contact with God praying for the two most important things for your life. The knowledge of God's will and that He would empower you to move straightaway into accomplishing His plan for your life. The main reason prayers don't get answered is because people don't pray–and people don't pray because they don't believe it works. If you pray outside of the scope of what you believe, or outside of the boundaries of your faith, you will not be successful. So you must put prayer into the right perspective. If you have never prayed in your life praying for tangible things probably is not a good place to start. Rather, pray for something that will allow you to see how God works inside of your heart and your life.

Overall, there are five necessary elements of prayer: the heart of prayer, the character of prayer, the agenda of prayer, the format of prayer, the seasons of prayer, and the motivation of prayer. Let's look at each one more closely:

The heart of prayer. You need to examine your heart when you decide to pray, and the heart of prayer is the intent you put forth. It actually is more important than the content of your prayers. The heart of prayer is the awareness that you don't really know how to pray and never will. Look at it this way: Once a person becomes adept at prayer the natural inclination is to become overconfident and self reliant. This is contrary to the very nature of prayer. Reaching out to have divine intervention in the affairs of life is a statement in and of itself that goes beyond human understanding. As a result, prayers limited to human understanding will always fall far short of God's best.

The character of prayer. Your character is who you are when no one else is around. It's the real you. It is the interpersonal place where the deep secrets of the soul reside. The character of prayer is that place in your prayers where you are hidden to the world and do not have to worry who knows what you are praying about. It is the secret place you share with God where you can reveal your deepest longings and greatest passions. God will answer you openly in matters that He sees and hears in secret.

The motivation of prayer. Most people are not motivated to pray by pure holy thoughts, just as I don't believe that people enter recovery because they saw the light. (I think people enter recovery because they felt the heat!) One of the biggest motivators for prayer is pain. People also pray when they are in fear. Often, when the fear, frustration, and pain are gone, so is the motivation to pray. That said, to last in recovery you need a spiritual awareness—an awareness of God and the fact that He helped you get free from alcohol, drugs and/or another addiction. Your prayer life needs to be motivated by more than negative emotions. It must be driven at a deep level that advances you from awareness to acceptance.

The agenda of prayer. It is clear that each person comes into recovery with his or her own motivations and desires. However, the key to an effective prayer life is to seek and find the agenda that God has for *your* life. God wants you to be successful as much as you want to succeed. God has a plan and will reveal the knowledge of His will for your life by showing you the agenda He has for your prayers. His agenda is always greater than yours.

The format of prayer. The most commonly used prayer in recovery is called the Lord's Prayer. Its format is important because it provides a structured map that can help you outline intentions. You may use formal prayer at times, and you also may pray in desperation about the matters in your life. Different methods will apply at different times, but you need to find your own balance as you embrace Step 11. Some pray in a very formal manner, while others are very unconventional. I have observed that this changes for people over time. Just remember that a ridged structure can sometimes squeeze the life out of your prayers, while a total lack of structure can cause your prayers to be scattered and inconsistent.

The seasons of prayer. As you become a student of prayer, you will find that there are clear variations, or seasons, within your prayer life. A time to cry, a time to laugh, a time to plant, and a time to reap, etc. Knowing that the seasons change will keep your prayer life fluid and help you avoid the tedium of a lifeless, faithless process without answers or responses from God.

In addition to these five components of prayer, there is an optional element called religious activities. Wherever there is a spiritual dimension of life, there are religious activities that stem from it. Churches are built around them, they are called particular denominations of faith, and while becoming religious can sometimes limit your growth, they can be very beneficial to building your spiritual life if kept in balance.

As you continue to strengthen your spiritual foundation, also be aware that there is a price tag on every relationship, whether divine or human, and it is the investment of time. When I began to invest time in my relationship with God I came to understand that once I had an awareness of God there were other levels on this spiritual journey that I must reach.

The first is called the **knowledge of God**. What I don't know or I don't understand about God cannot come into play anymore. The only things that count are the truths that I do understand. I know

He loves me. He is not mad at me. He is not out to get me. God is all powerful. I know this because everything that I have asked God to remove from my life he has removed, and He answers all of my prayers.

The next level is **communication with God** because no relationship can grow without interaction. The loneliness that addicts and alcoholics experience is not the absence of people in their lives. It is the absence of communication. When you stop interacting you will fall back into loneliness. This is not a monologue. Prayer and meditation are talking to God and hearing from Him, respectively. It is a dialogue that goes on all the time.

When you reach the place where you have communication, you develop an **intimacy with God**. This is the place where God reveals to you how much He loves you. When I attained an intimacy with God, I found the pathway to a genuine relationship with Him. In that place I recognize that God has a plan and a purpose for my life, and it is for me to be successful. Now I can talk to God about anything. When people fall into error and make mistakes, they often get depressed and confused and never bring it up in prayer. However, when I experience these emotions I know they are just barometers of where I am when I enter into prayer, and they are the first things I talk about with God. There is nothing that comes into my life good, bad, or indifferent that I cannot address with God.

This relationship develops an honest **expectation of God**. I have a reasonable belief that when God gives me something He puts it in my heart as a direction, as a plan that He is going to help me fulfill. When you expect something from God it activates God's expectation of you. God expects you to do certain things and act in a certain way. The closer you get to God and the longer you walk with God, the more responsibility you have. God expects a lot of things. "From him who has been given much, much is required," (Luke 12:48).

This leads to the next level of relationship, which is **trust in God**. You cannot trust God without knowing Him and understanding the interface of relational expectations. It is the same with people. When you build interpersonal bonds, you know what to expect from them and they know what to expect from you. For example, when I walk in that bond of trust with God I know that He always will intervene when I need help. God always answers my prayers, particularly when I'm in trouble and not thinking straight. God will never override my free will, but the moment that I ask Him to empower my free will to make the right choices it is done.

The last step in this process is **worship**. This draws your focus **to God** because whatever you focus on becomes bigger in your life. If you continually focus on drinking and drugs than they are going to become bigger than anything else in your life. Prayer and meditation can help alter this cycle. Remember, prayer is communication with God. Meditation is what you think about and hear from God. If you incorporate both of these spiritual practices into your life I can assure that God will be with you. I have that much trust. In closing consider the following story as it relates to the principle awareness of God.

During The Great Depression there was a boy who lived out in the Midwest in a dustbowl farm where money was almost nonexistent. One day the boy heard on the old radio that the circus was coming to town, and all he could think about was going to see the show.

The boy asked his father, "Dad, do you think I can go to the circus?"

"It's a couple of months before the circus comes to town," he replied. "If you work hard and we can save up our pennies I will make sure that you have a quarter to go to town."

So they worked diligently all during that next season. Then the day came that the circus arrived. The little boy got a sack lunch and his quarter, and he headed off to see the show. He got to the town just as the big train was rolling in, and he could see it coming. A crowd had gathered around as the different colored cars went by. He could see all the animals painted on the sides. The workers started opening up the cars and out came lions, tigers, elephants, and giraffes. There were clowns, and people balancing plates and riding on unicycles. The boy just stood there absorbing all these wonderful things that he had only dreamed about.

After all the animals and performers had filed into the tent, the little boy went up to the man at the entrance and said, "I've been here watching this circus and I don't know who takes my quarter."

The man said, "You give it to me."

The man took the boy's quarter and the boy took his program and he headed off on the long walk back to his house. When he got back he told his father all about the circus and what he saw: lions, tigers, and elephants coming off the train; clowns in costumes; and the unicycles.

His father asked, "What did you think when you went into the tent?"

The little boy said he didn't go into the tent, he saw the show outside. His father just turned away with a tear in his eye because he knew the boy went to the circus, had seen some things, but he had missed the main event and he didn't even know it.

You can go to meetings, you can get accumulated time sober, you can get a sponsor, and you can read all the literature you can find on recovery. However, if you don't establish a relationship with God, you are missing the main event.

KEYSTONES OF BUILDING A CONTINUAL CONNECTION WITH GOD

Awareness of God. Knowing there is a God leads to an acceptance of Him. Little by little God reveals Himself to you. There is a price tag on the relationship and it is the investment of time in prayer and meditation. Time is the great equalizer in all spiritual life. It is the one thing every person is given in equal share. How you invest it will determine how much conscious contact you have with God.

Knowledge of God. What you don't know or understand about God cannot come into play in the development of your spiritual life. You need to know a person before you can relate to him or her and understand what to expect. The same is true of God. Saying you do not know anything about God will make it impossible for Him to intervene in your life.

Communication with God. No relationship, either human or divine, can grow without communication. Talking to God and listening to God is the only way to know that He is always with you. Practice communication with God and your spiritual bond will strengthen.

Intimacy with God. By attaining an intimacy with God, you recognize that He has a plan and a purpose for your life, and it is for you to be successful. There is nothing that comes into your life good, bad, or indifferent that you cannot address in prayer.

Relationship with God. By building a relationship with God, you can develop honest expectations of Him. An expectation of God will activate God's expectations of you. God will know that you are ready to help others, to give of your time, and to stay away from the wrong people, places, and things.

Trust in God. You cannot trust God without knowing Him and understanding the interface of relational expectations. When you walk in a bond of trust with God you know that he always will intervene when you need help.

Worship God. Actively worshiping draws your focus to God. Whatever you focus on becomes bigger in your life, so you need to take your mind from your addiction and place it on improving your conscious contact with God.

A newlywed couple that hadn't been intimate yet went on their honeymoon. At the hotel, the new bride was sitting on the edge of the bed and she was concerned because she had the worst breath of anyone she knew. So far she had been masking it with mints, but she knew there was going to be no way to hide it now. Meanwhile, the new groom was sitting in the bathroom on the edge of the tub in a terrible dilemma because he had the worst foot odor of anybody that ever lived. He didn't know how to tell his wife. He was just sitting in there, and a long time went by.

Finally she called, "Are you going to come out?"

He said, "I will be right out."

So he came walking out timidly and she got up, walked over, and got right up in front of him. She looked at him in the face and said, "I have something I need to admit to you."

He replied, "Don't tell me you ate my socks!"

CHAPTER 12

SERVICE

One time I was going to help a man get into an addictions recovery program that I was running. He had to attend some type of treatment program or he was going to land in prison. When he was in court to receive sentencing, I showed up and I told the judge about the program I was running. The judge recognized the program.

The judge said, "I know about you. Is he going to come into your program?"

I said, "Yes sir. If you will let him, he will come to my program."

The judge turned to the man and said, "You are going to go over to Dr. Sutton's program, and you are going to do everything he tells you to do. If you don't make it in that program, you don't even get to come back and talk to me. They are going to handcuff you and drive you straight to the receiving facility at the prison. Then you are going to do all six years of your time. Do you understand that?"

The guy said, "Yes sir."

So we came out of the courtroom and started talking. My program was only about four blocks from the courthouse. I told him I would give him a ride down there, but he said his girlfriend was there and they were going to follow me in her car. I said fine, and when I got to my office I started talking on the phone. Later I noticed that a lot of time had passed and he wasn't there. Three hours later, I called the judge on his cell phone and said he didn't show.

He didn't turn up for three days! Needless to say, the police took him to prison when he finally arrived at my door. I got the judge to hear me, but this man was dumb enough to think that he was smarter than everyone and didn't have to listen to what I said or do what needed to be done. That clearly was not the way to establish a relationship with a person trying to help through service work in recovery.

Unfortunately, this is the way many people in early recovery try to approach the relationship with a sponsor. They want the benefits of the association without putting in the effort to follow the necessary directions to actually begin the process of getting well and whole. Those who fall into this trap miss out on one of the most transforming and gratifying experiences in recovery.

> **Step 12:** *Having had a spiritual awakening as a result of these steps, we tried to carry this message to alcoholics, and to practice these principles in all our affairs.*

 # PRINCIPLE: SERVICE

Service to others involves relationships. Unfortunately, people with addictions usually aren't big on helping others or good at relationships. I know when I was an active alcoholic, service to *me* was about as far as I got. It was the quick-fix mentality that I have mentioned so many times in these pages. I didn't really care what happened to you unless it had some affect on what was going to happen to me. And if that was the case, I could be very nice to you providing I got something out of it.

We know that addicts are focused on themselves and these traits are at the core of their predicament. The first 11 Chapters have been focused primarily on taking an inventory and finding a way out of this addictive mindset. Chapter 12 actually is the acid test for this process. You are going to see if you have broken the cycle by determining if you can reach out and help other people.

If you cannot successfully undertake the process of helping others, you will be destined to repeat some part of the cycle of addiction again. Maybe you have been through half a dozen programs and you are wondering why you haven't gotten it yet. It's probably because you were in those programs working on *your* agenda, focusing on what you wanted to do, identifying which rules you thought you could get around because you believed you were above those rules. You thought you were the one person who was exempt from following the directions. And the pattern that you developed in *your* treatment programs went with you right out the door every time you left—and it wasn't very long until you discovered that your methods failed once again.

The way that you can determine whether or not you have broken through self-centeredness and greediness is by evaluating your ability to give. People who are greedy and hoarding, people who capture it all for themselves and refuse to give anything back to others, cannot break through addiction. You probably have heard the phrase "you have to give it away to keep it." It is true! It means that in order to keep what you have achieved in sobriety, you have to find somebody who needs what you have, and then you must give it away to him or her.

Obviously, you can't share something that you haven't acquired. You actually need to attain some form of quality sobriety before you can help other people. I have said this before and it bears repeating: There is a really thin line between carrying the message and spreading the disease. Hence, you need to make sure you have a message to share. You need to be clear that you have made a connection with God and that you are not just talking about some superficial concept that does not empower you to do anything.

Having a spiritual connection personally is necessary to help anyone make a spiritual connection themselves. I definitely had a spiritual awakening as I walked through this process. I came into a relationship with God. I am aware and cognizant that there is a spiritual life that is attached to everything that I do. The next thing we do is to attempt to take this sober life to those addicted and to activate these principles in everything we do. What is the message? This message is that we have become spiritually aware. As a Christian it is the message that there is hope and forgiveness through Christ. There is freedom from addiction and restoration for every part of my life. I will have it as soon as I decide to let my old ideas fall away. I will keep it as long as I am willing to begin to help others. This is service to others. Freely I have received freely I should give.

I believe service to others primarily is about sponsorship and entering into a relationship where you commit to another person to help him or her individually. The real deal is when you have made a commitment to another human being in a one-to-one relationship. It doesn't matter if you are playing the role of the sponsor or the sponsee; in both cases you are helping another in recovery. In the three decades that I have been sober I have allowed 36 different people live in my house. I also want to tell you that I am 100 percent successful with everybody I sponsor. I don't know if any of those individuals are sober now, but I am—and that makes me successful. Actually I know the fruit that remains very well and there is a lot!

Overall, there are different levels of sponsorship relationships, and each type forms a unique expression that blends two personalities. There is no one size-fits-all approach to this process. Being aware of this will prevent wrong expectations, which is the primary reason for failure. Hence, when you go into a sponsorship relationship as either a sponsor or sponsee you need to clarify your expectations of each other at the front end and define the type of relationship you will establish. Here are the different levels you need to recognize as a sponsee:

Intense. Whenever you start into a new sponsorship relationship it should be intense. You should be talking on the phone every day and seeing each other at meetings. You should have a sponsor who attends your home group. Get a home group and then get a sponsor from that home group, and show up at that home group every time the door is open. Do these things and you probably will stay sober.

Calling every day is important, even if you don't have anything to say. Why? It's because you need to develop a habit of talking to other people. If you do not do this you will not have a support system in place when you get into a bad spot and start thinking about going back into your addiction. I was told early on to call my sponsor if I thought I was going to drink. I thought that was the stupidest thing I ever heard. You probably will feel the same way in early sobriety. Don't fall into that trap. Call and leave a message if he or she is not there so you will get into the habit of doing it. From the other end, it will allow your sponsor to get to know you well, so that on the day you are feeling off he or she can spot it a mile away and see the red flags going up.

Intimate. Over time, a sponsor/sponsee relationship will move from intense to intimate and become almost family-like. Your sponsor will become acquainted with what you do on a daily basis. He or she might know where you work, know your kids' names, and understand your problems and complaints. At this level, you learn how to communicate and understand each other's sense of humor.

Active. An active relationship is when you know what is going on in another person's life in recovery, and you share his or her problems, challenges, victories, and goals. It is a secondary sponsorship role that is ongoing. In this level of relationship, you may see your sponsor at meetings and even meet with regularity. This probably is the most common type of sponsor relationship you will have as you move forward in sobriety.

Casual. In a casual sponsorship model, you don't see your sponsor much or talk frequently. It may be a long-distance relationship or one that has lasted for many years. I have this type of relationship with my sponsor, who I have worked with for more than 25 years. I visit him occasionally and we catch up every few months. This is a low-maintenance relationship. There also is a second form of casual sponsorship where your sponsor never gets to know much about your life. It may be somebody in your home group that you see only at meetings, but you always inquire about each other's recovery and progress.

Distant. These are very informal relationships where you might recognize somebody by face but not even know his or her name. It is that person you know from a meeting, run into later, and say hello in passing. It's recognizing others in your fellowship and greeting them with kindness and care.

After you have worked the helping others deal for a period of time and mastered the principles, you will reach a point where you are both a sponsee and a sponsor. At this point there are several things you need to know about each role that you will take on. First, let's look at what you need to know about working with others as a sponsor.

You can't force people to learn if they do not want to learn. People may agree with you and say they are going to take what you suggest and change; however, they will not learn beyond their willingness to actually apply what is being offered.

You cannot answer questions that people don't ask. You might know what questions somebody should be asking, but if you bring something up without a question being posed first you will be talking to deaf ears. When someone asks a question it shows a preparedness to listen to what you have to say.

You cannot help anyone who feels you are unqualified to help him or her. A person who selects a sponsor under the assumption that he or she is smarter than the teacher is an idiot. Remember that the man who sponsors himself has a fool for a sponsor.

You cannot learn without repetition. You must go over things with a sponsee more than one time. You must hear something six times for it to register with you. As a result, you must be patient and persistent when working with others to get the message through.

Now let's switch gears and look at the steps you will have to take when finding the right sponsor for yourself.

To get a sponsor you must ask somebody! I know this is a big step, but don't stop if somebody turns you down. If you ask someone to be your sponsor and he (or she) says no, ask if that person can direct you to someone who can be your sponsor. Do you know how I got my sponsor? I asked a man whom I admired to help me.

Ability is not the same as availability. You can go to home groups where the chairperson will say, "Anybody who is here who is willing to be a sponsor raise your hand." People then reluctantly put their hands up. Those are the ones that you probably don't want to approach to become your sponsor! The best way to find somebody who has the ability to be your sponsor is to listen to what people in meetings have to say. If someone says something that you connect with, he (or she) might be a good sponsor for you. Don't just pick a person because he raised his hand at a meeting. While both ability and availability are necessary, the ability to communicate with you in a way that *you* can understand is imperative.

Pick a sponsor that you are drawn to be around. Does he or she have what you want? If you are a single mom with three children living on a limited income and you are having trouble paying your bills, I'm not sure that finding someone who has been retired for 30 years who has more money than she knows what to do with can relate to you. You need to find somebody who can identify with what you are going through. If you have been in prison, for example, you might want to find somebody who has been in prison because there are some specific things that a man or woman coming out of this situation will face that other people have not faced, will not face, and will not be able to understand. Ask God who is the best person to serve as your sponsor. You can do more than pray after you have prayed, but you cannot do more than pray until you have prayed. I believe that God can provide you with the perfect sponsor if you ask. Select someone who is in your pathway of life or recovery.

What are the makings of a great sponsor? From a recovery perspective, there are two ways in life to get wisdom. One way is to discover what is right through your own mistakes. The other is to get an outstanding sponsor! When you learn from your mistakes you learn the wrong way of doing something. There is a better way, and that is through the knowledge of others.

Great sponsors transfer sobriety through relationships, and over time you may recognize many different perspectives. Your similarity to another person may not be as important as your points of difference. Celebrate your differences. The points where you are not alike will create the necessary exposure to the things you really need to change. Great sponsors know how to demonstrate through their lives what you need to change to become whole.

Great sponsors guarantee their information. If you have practiced something and it works, you can be sure it will work for somebody else. I don't practice what I preach, I preach what I practice. I only will take a sponsee down the road that I have been down. I don't read something out of a book one week and then teach it in a class the next week. I live what I teach others. As a result, I know what works and what does not work.

Great sponsors can establish possibility. If you don't use your gifts, whatever they are in life, you will lose them. An outstanding sponsor can look into a person's heart and see his or her potential and then help to nurture it. This is not just about giving up drinking or using drugs. This is about helping someone to find true meaning in life.

Great sponsors can stop the adversary. First, they can help sponsees identify their enemies. Maybe the enemy is bad relationships, where a person goes from one destructive relationship to another. Additionally, they can help paralyze people that don't like a sponsee by stepping in and supporting him or her in a time of need or attack.

Great sponsors can get the right people to listen. That could be a future employer or a judge. Maybe it's a family member. I've talked to some irate spouses in my time!

Great sponsors require quest for recovery. A good sponsor does not chase a sponsee around, and a wise sponsor never works harder than the sponsee at that individual's recovery. The message from the sponsor should be: "If you want what I have, you must come do what I do." I like the passage of scripture where the Apostle Paul says, "Follow me as I follow Christ." Paul didn't say, "follow Christ." He said, "follow me as I follow Christ."

Great sponsors are more interested in a sponsee's achievement than his or her fondness. The focus should be on correction rather than celebration. I hope my sponsees like me, but I am more interested in them getting well and achieving long-term sobriety than whether or not they enjoy my company.

Great sponsors are not necessarily sponsees' best friends. Your best friend loves you the way you are; your sponsor loves you too much to leave you the way you are. Your best friend is comfortable with your past; your sponsor is comfortable with your future. Your best friend ignores your weaknesses; your sponsor removes your weaknesses. Your best friend is your cheerleader; your sponsor is your coach. Your best friend sees what you do right; your sponsor sees what you do wrong and is not afraid to tell you about it.

Great sponsors see things before sponsees do. An outstanding sponsor has already experienced the pain that a sponsee is about to create. He or she will say, "I've already done that, and it's going to hurt real bad! You go ahead and do that, and I will be here for you to cry on my shoulder."

Great sponsors produce great sponsees. What your sponsor believes and knows is important because he (or she) will teach you how to operate in the way that mirrors his (or her) life. Then you take what you have learned, embrace it, and build your own pathway. Now you have something valuable to pass on to other people, even though you might not be as good at something as your sponsor is. That doesn't matter because you might be better at something else that your sponsor is not very good at doing.

If you embrace the principle of Service to Others you can become a mentor to somebody else. You can step into others' lives and teach them what you know. Note, however, that sponsees will withdraw from you when they refuse to admit their errors, when they feel their goals and directions are superior to yours, and when you express disappointment in their progress. You need to take everything in stride and work through it.

The ultimate goal in sponsorship is to convey a lifestyle of sobriety. This can only happen if the sponsee puts himself or herself in a position to learn. If you are working harder than the sponsee you are not helping. You are enabling that person to remain the same. From the other side of the street, here's what it takes to become an outstanding sponsee.

The ideal sponsee is an passionate learner. Get excited about what your sponsor can teach you. Learn from his or her mistakes and save yourself from unnecessary pain in your recovery journey.

An outstanding sponsee should be willing to make sacrifices to be in the company of the sponsor. You should sacrifice your schedule and your time to posture yourself to spend time with your sponsor. If you are struggling in recovery it is proof that you have not accepted that you need assistance from others. You are still fighting, and you are doing it on your own!

The successful sponsee follows the guidance of a sponsor. A sponsor cannot correct what you are not willing to confront. What you fail to destroy in your life ultimately will destroy you. I hear people say sponsors are not supposed to counsel people. Well, what are they supposed to do? I know a sponsor is not a licensed counselor, but when a sponsor opens his (or her) mouth and shares experience, strength, and hope, he (or she) is giving counsel to a person in need. A sponsor must be confident enough to stand behind his (or her) advice.

A stellar sponsee should freely discuss his or her pain and mistakes with a sponsor. All men fall, but great ones get back up. So when you fall you need to get up immediately. If you are not open and honest with your sponsor, then when you fall you are not going to be able to discuss it. And when addicted people can't address problems, they go back out and relapse.

A great sponsee reveals the imaginings and wishes of his or her heart. What you are willing to walk away from will determine what God is willing to bring to you. Do you really want something new? Do you want to move to a new dimension? What are you willing to walk away from? The price of spiritual progress is obedience to the will of God. What is God's will? If you did Step 11 then you already know that.

The ideal sponsee clearly defines expectations. A smart sponsee uses the shelter of a sponsor during times of attack and turmoil. I know people that stay on their sponsor's couch when it gets really tough. They do whatever it takes to stay sober for another day, because recovery is one day at a time.

A great sponsee gladly gives back into the life of a sponsor. For example, he or she will willingly jump into activities in which the sponsor participates, including groups, special events, and even other service work.

While sponsorship is indeed the foundation of Step 12, to stay on solid ground in recovery you need to be aware that not all people are going to be perfect sponsees. The three types of sponsees that can cause you difficulty are passive, freeloader, and prodigal. Passive sponsees reach out only when it's convenient and their personal efforts have not produced the desired results. Freeloader sponsees pursue for standing, not rectification. They want to use the name and influence of the sponsor to manipulate other people. They want what the sponsor has earned, not learned. They want the sponsor's reputation in sobriety. Parasitic sponsors will drain the life out of you. Prodigal sponsees, on the other hand, enter and exit a relationship freely. When serious direction is given or correction occurs they move on to another sponsor who doesn't know their flaws.

A high level of connection, the right friends, the right associations, and the right people will bring out the original personality in you—the one that God gave to you. The wrong people will bring out the worst in you and your ego, and you should never discuss your problems with someone incapable of contributing to the solution. Not everyone has the right to speak into your life. Finding the appropriate sponsor and identifying sponsees who you can personally connect with and help are key components of a successful recovery program. The *Big Book* of Alcoholics Anonymous emphasizes Step 12 and the principle of service saying, "There is nothing that will so much insure immunity from the next drink as intensive work with other alcoholics."

The whole premise of the recovery process is twofold: to get better and to help others. "Freely ye have received, freely give." (Matthew 10:8) There is no clearer instruction on the concept of service. Recovery is a gift from God, by grace. There is no one who can afford it and no one who can buy it. It's not for sale because it's free. And what's more, the only way that you can keep it is to give it away. The very moment you begin to take credit for what only God could have done, you begin to lose what you have.

The essence of the "spiritual awakening" that you will receive by working through the process is that you will know it is a gift given to you to give to others. Certainly you have been enlightened of God's love through this process. Surely you have seen your mistakes and taken corrective action. Without a doubt, you are never going to be perfect, but in your journey hopefully you have realized that God in His infinite mercy has made you a productive member of society by providing you with a way to help others. The key to your own recovery and happiness is found through reaching out to those who are still suffering.

"This is my commandment, that ye love one another, as I have loved you. Greater love hath no man than this, that a man lay down his life for his friends." (John 15:12,13).

As you attempt to help others you are able to see the pain and destruction of your old lifestyle. This in itself often is enough to keep the average person on the right track in sobriety. But the principle of service goes beyond even this. Regardless what you give out of your life, it will be returned back to you multiple times. Unfortunately, many who have found their way into an understanding of God have never come to this realization and they are missing out. Often their relationships are lacking faith, hope, charity, or love. They can be easily disillusioned because they have fixed their eyes on what they want, and not the needs of others.

Using the principles of recovery in all of your affairs is a lifelong process. It doesn't say practice these steps in all our affairs, but practice these principles. If you will help others, God will help you. He will use others to bring your life into balance and the fullness of His joy.

THE TOP 10 QUALITIES OF A GREAT SPONSOR

There are two ways to get wisdom.

No. 1: *Discover what is right through your own mistakes.*

No. 2: *Get a great sponsor.*

TOP 10 QUALITIES OF GREAT SPONSORS:

1. Transfer insight through relationships.
2. Certify their information.
3. Determine your future.
4. Protect you from adversary.
5. Connect you with people who will listen to you.
6. Require your quest.
7. Are more interested in your achievement than your affection.
8. Are not necessarily your best friend.
9. See things that will cause you pain before you do.
10. Produce great sponsees.

CPSIA information can be obtained at www.ICGtesting.com
Printed in the USA
241330LV00002B/4/P